GAMES

MAGAZINE PRESENTS

BRAIN TWISTERS

from the

WORLD PUZZLE CHAMPIONSHIPS

VOLUME 3

EDITED BY WILL SHORTZ
AND RON OSHER

TIMES
T
BOOKS

All rights reserved under International and Pan-American Copyright Conventions.
Published in the United States by Times Books, a division of Random House, Inc.,
New York, and simultaneously in Canada by Random House of Canada Limited, Toronto.

ISBN 0-8129-2940-3

Random House Puzzle Website Address:
http://www.puzzlesatrandom.com/

Page design and typography by Mark Frnka

Manufactured in the United States of America

9 8 7 6 5 4 3 2

First Edition

CONTENTS

CONTENTS

FOREWORD

The victorious Team USA at the 1996 World Puzzle Championships at Utrecht. From left: Wei-Hwa Huang, Ron Osher, Zack Butler, Nick Baxter, and team captain Will Shortz.

Team Results

Top 10 Teams – 1995		Top 10 Teams – 1996	
1 USA	17463	1 USA	3013
2 Czech Rep.	17305	2 Czech Rep.	2557
3 Hungary	16250	3 Turkey	2149
4 Romania	15979	4 Netherlands	2135
5 Turkey	14992	5 Poland	1933
6 Germany	13995	6 Russia	1872
7 Croatia	13926	7 Germany	1840
8 Russia	12516	8 Japan	1726
9 Japan	12187	9 Hungary	1657
10 Netherlands	12066	10 Slovakia	1638

Individual Results

Top 10 Individuals – 1995

1	Wei-Hwa Huang	USA
2	György Istvan	Hungary
3	Pavel Kalhous	Czech Rep.
4	Zack Butler	USA
5	Ron Osher	USA
6	Petr Vejchoda	Czech Rep.
7	Markus Gegenheimer	Germany
8	Kresz Karoly	Hungary
9	Robert Babilon	Czech Rep.
10	Pero Galogaza	Croatia

Top 10 Individuals – 1996

1	Robert Babilon	Czech Rep.
2	Zack Butler	USA
3	Wei-Hwa Huang	USA
4	Pavel Kalhous	Czech Rep.
5	Ron Osher	USA
6	Paul Jacobs	Netherlands
7	Nick Baxter	USA
8	Markus Gegenheimer	Germany
9	Petr Nepovim	Czech Rep.
10	Güray Erus	Turkey

Team USA is basking in its glory after the 4th and 5th World Puzzle Championships, 1995-96, finishing first among the world's best puzzle solvers both years.

This annual event, as you may know from previous volumes in this series, joins puzzlers from many countries solving a battery of diversely original language- and culture-neutral puzzles.

Founded in New York in 1992, the WPC is held in a different city each year. The 4th took place in the rustic mountain resort of Poiana Brasov, Romania. The 5th was held in Utrecht, the Netherlands. The hosts supply the puzzles. It is their duty to ensure that the puzzles are not only innovative and enjoyable, but also as free of language and cultural bias as possible. Thus, there are no standard crosswords or other puzzles that involve answering clues in a particular language. Instead, solvers face tests of logic, mathematical ability, spatial skills, observation, memory, etc.

This volume contains the best puzzles from the two most recent championships. The 1995 puzzles are presented with permission from Ovidiu Sperlea and Cristea Ionita of *Ecran* magazine. The 1996 puzzles are by the staff of Puzzelsport magazines, under the editorship of Rob Geensen. You'll find such traditional favorites here as Battleships, Minesweeper, Cross Sums, crisscrosses, and mazes, as well as new puzzle varieties of all sorts.

I would like to thank Stanley Newman and Times Books for providing the U.S. team with the financial support each year to compete. Also Lufthansa German Airlines for providing international travel. And acknowledgments to team member Ron Osher, the 1994 world champion individual solver, for selecting and editing puzzles for the book.

Whether or not you're a world-class-caliber solver, the following divertissements are bound to keep your mind pleasantly occupied.

And if you secretly think you are world-class ... well, let us know. There may be a future WPC team spot available for you!

Will Shortz
U.S. Team Captain

FOURTH WORLD PUZZLE CHAMPIONSHIP

The 1995 Championship was held in Brasov, Romania and like every World Puzzle Championship, the competition was intended to be laguage and culture neutral. While participants came from locations as diverse as Japan, Croatia, Canada and Russia, the languages used for some of the puzzles were even more unexpected. Understanding all of the words wasn't important, but we were nevertheless confronted by puzzles with entries in Albanian, Swedish, German, French, Italian, English, Dutch, Spanish and Turkish. And now, so are you!

Besides the language(s), you may find some of the other aspects of international competition unusual as well:

- Crossword grids are not necessarily symmetrical.

- Unchecked letters and two letter "words" are commonplace

Most importantly of all, you will see a variety of puzzles, problems and challenges not found in any puzzle book or magazine anywhere.

CAPITAL CITIES TOUR

A	A	B	C	E	N	R	R	W
A	A	B	E	I	I	L	R	S
G	I	K	L	N	N	O	S	T
E	H	L	M	N	N	O	P	P
A	I	I	M	N	O	O	R	V
A	C	I	N	N	N	O	S	U
A	A	G	G	I	N	O	S	T
E	H	I	I	K	L	N	S	T
E	E	F	N	O	O	R	T	W
A	E	I	N	O	P	R	R	T

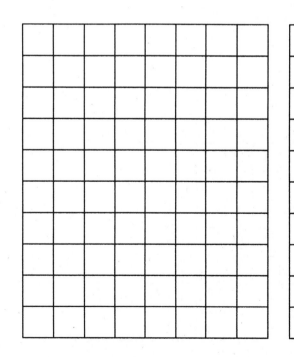

WHAT'S THE POINT

To solve this puzzle, place an arrow in each square of the border so that the number appearing in each box matches the number of arrows pointed at that box.

3	3	6	2	3
5	4	3	2	4
5	2	2	0	3
2	2	3	0	2
4	3	5	3	6

Example:

↘	↙	↓	↙	↓	
→	4	3	4	1	4	↙
↗	1	1	4	0	3	↘
→	5	2	4	5	5	←
→	3	3	5	3	6	←
→	2	2	5	1	3	↘
	↑	↗	↑	↖	↑

GEO-LOGICAL

Place the indicated letter into the row or column according to the number given. Where more than one number appears, the letter appears more than once, separated by at least one other letter. Fill in the grid completely using your knowledge of geography as well as logic.

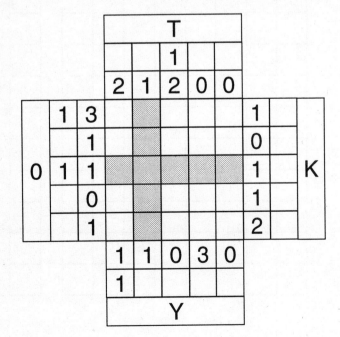

Example:

		A				
		1				
	1	0	1	2	0	
	0	B	C	A	B	C	1	1
	2	B	B	D	D	C	2
D	2 1	C	D	D	B	D	1	B
	0	A	C	B	A	B	1	1
	1	C	C	A	A	D	0
		1	1	0	0	2
		1	2
		C

8

INTRODUCTION TO ALBANIAN

By correctly eliminating one letter from each word, you can be the first on your block to solve a crossword in Albanian.

ACROSS

1 ZBULMET
6 ULETM
9 ARGAB
10 ROCL
12 RHA
13 RAKINTIK
16 EHT
17 ZEMWËRUAR
19 LËAROJ
21 RKEM
22 BUT
24 CVEM
26 MEMËRORE
28 AQU
30 BUBUREK
31 TADNI
33 ALN
34 DECËS
36 RUZAJTJE
39 HUTA
41 KIKI
42 NOTFAR

DOWN

1 BARESLË
2 URAKTË
3 PLAK
4 MBIZGOTËROJ
5 TIRIM
6 JUL
7 EPH
8 EMARRË
11 POKËR
14 TREJ
15 DULME
18 RESCETË
20 RUMYB
23 HOKTEJ
25 OMAN
26 ECUNUK
27 RKE
29 QILARQ
30 BGARI
32 SASHT
35 CREN
37 AIO
38 STI
40 UJA

9

HOW COORDINATED ARE YOU?

The Swedish words from the list below must be inserted into the diagram in such a way that the number of letters in each horizontal and vertical line corresponds to the "coordinate" attached to it. No letter appears more than once in any row or column.

A	HA	FET	HEAT
F	SI	FUR	HUSA
H	UH	TEG	RISA
S		TRI	GIFTE

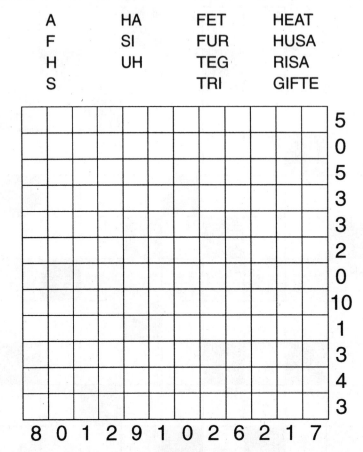

5
0
5
3
3
2
0
10
1
3
4
3

8 0 1 2 9 1 0 2 6 2 1 7

Example:

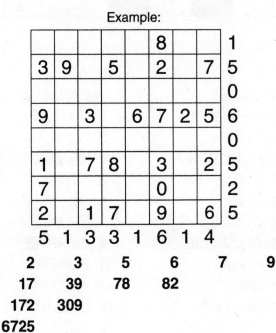

				8			1
3	9		5		2		7	5
							0
9		3		6	7	2	5	6
							0
1		7	8		3		2	5
7					0			2
2		1	7		9		6	5

5 1 3 3 1 6 1 4

2	3	5	6	7	9
17	39	78	82		
172	309				
6725					

10

FIGURE IT OUT

Fill in the grid using each number exactly once.
Numbers may only be entered from left to right or top to bottom.

3:	4:	5:
157	1817	27916
228	2565	47566
297	3147	52396
325	4332	92136
416	5841	
486	6239	
541	6364	
673	6510	
750	7156	
762	9896	
991		

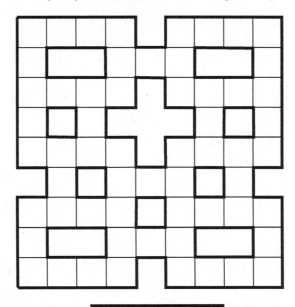

Example:

2 48, 84
4 3775, 3776, 6158, 7785

BATTLE-MINE-SWEEPER-SHIPS

As in regular battleships, you must fit the shapes shown (the ships) into the diagram given (the ocean). As in regular minesweepers, the numbers in the grid tell you how many horizontally or vertically (but not diagonally) adjacent squares are occupied. Unlike regular battleships, ships may touch each other diagonally (see example).

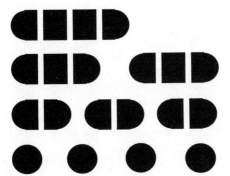

Example:

SOMETHING FOR EVERYONE

ACROSS

1 American scientist, inventor of the telephone
4 British physicist who introduced the temperature scale which bears his name
8 Symphony #3, Opus 55 by Ludwig van Beethoven
10 Device which produces an intense beam of light of a very pure single color
11 Prefix meaning "weight," "pressure"
13 High English nobility title
14 Artificial international language created by L. Zamenhof
16 The administrative capital city of the South African Republic
19 Ancient center of civilization in southern Mesopotamia
21 Annual movie prize awarded in Hollywood
22 First league soccer club from Neuchâtel (Switzerland)
25 Central institution of U.S. intelligence
26 American writer, author of "Last of the Mohicans"
29 French seafarer of the XVII century, protagonist of battles against England
31 Czech composer of the symphony "From the New World"
33 The capital city of Bulgaria, situated on the site of the ancient Roman colony Serdica
36 Northwestern U.S. state
37 Japanese Prime Minister from the epoch of the great reforms (Hirobumi)
39 The chemical symbol of the element tantalum
40 American actor and singer of "White Christmas"

DOWN

1 Economic and customs union established by Belgium, the Netherlands and Luxembourg
2 The god of love in Greek mythology, son of Aphrodite
3 African state in the Gulf of Guinea, founded in 1822 by former Afro-American slaves
4 Japanese self-defense technique without arms
5 Royal dynasty and province (former dukedom) in France
6 The abbreviation of the International Organization for Standardization
7 Roman emperor, initiator of the anti-Christian persecutions (Claudius Drusu Germanicus)
9 The abbreviation of the Cooperative for American Remittances to Europe, a charity organization from the USA
12 John Lennon's second wife
15 Musical notation for "too much"
17 The capital city of Ghana
18 Country where Farsi is spoken
20 The king of Thailand, ascended to the throne in 1946
23 American inventor, builder of the telegraph
24 Variable explosive star with suddenly amplifying brightness
27 The supreme divinity in (North) Germanic mythology
28 The Muse of erotic poetry in Greek mythology
29 French physicist with contributions in the field of magnetism
30 State in western Africa with the capital city of Lomé
32 Premature victory in a boxing match (abbr.)
34 English reformer, the founder of the Quaker sect
35 German writer, the author of the novels from the "Winnetou" series
38 The chemical symbol of the element osmium

DO RE MI

Fit the German words into the grid in the row and columns indicated.
Then identify the musical celebrity who lived between the years shown.
(You can look it up!)

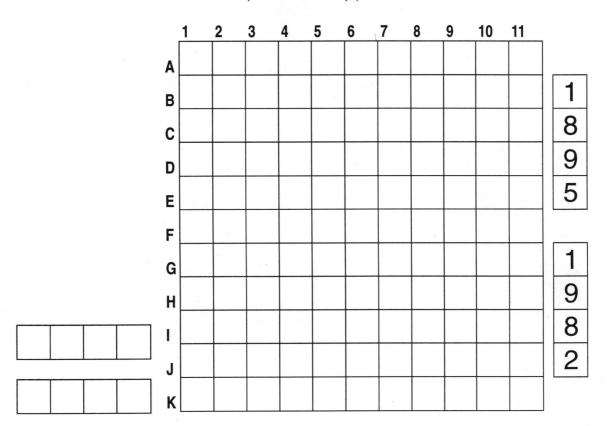

A GI, IRR, KOPF		**1** ICHTHYOLOGE
B COLT, TULPEN		**2** FT, ROSA, TJA
C AU, HS, PAARE		**3** ETA, RL, UH
D SPUR, TAUB		**4** SCHI, TABAK
E HALTE, TOT		**5** LASCHE
F KAI, SEE, YT		**6** OT, STICH, UM
G OJE, SCHURKE		**7** PUPPE
H FRON, LATSCH		**8** FLAU, SUFFIX
I ACH, OFEN		**9** PARTERRE
J GF, HEU, OB		**10** GER, OEKONOM
K ETUI, MAXIME		**11** BE, EN, INERT

DIVISION OF LABOR

Divide the diagram into twelve numbered sections of equal size and shape.
The shapes may be rotations and/or reflections of each other.

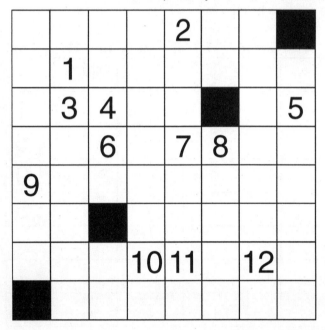

Example:

URBAN SKYLINE

The diagram below represents 36 square blocks of an urban landscape. The numbers on
the borders indicate how many different buildings can be seen from that vantage point.
No row or column contains two buildings of the same height. All the buildings are
from 1 to 6 stories tall. Fill in the grid, with the heights of the missing buildings.

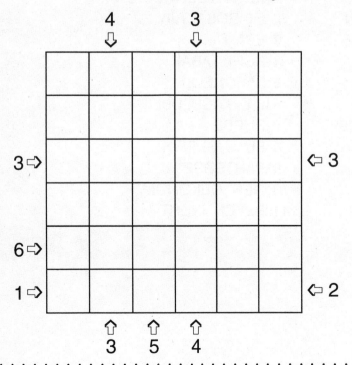

Example:

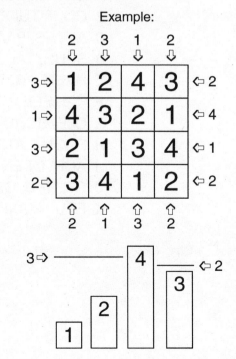

A NEUTRAL PUZZLE

Fill in the grid with the French, Italian and German words listed.
(Diacritical marks may be ignored.) Then color the diagram appropriately.

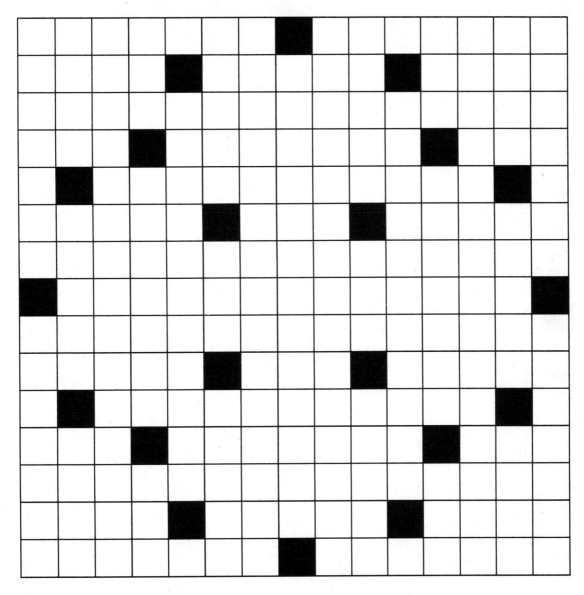

2 AD, AV, EH, HÉ, LA, LE, LO, NE, NO, ON, OR, RE, SO, ST, TU, UR

3 ALA, ÂNE, COC, LOG, PER, POT, ROI, VIA

4 ARDU, ASEN, ASUL, ÉCOT, ÉTAT, FRAU, GENE, GOGO, IDOL, NOCE, ODEN, ODER, OPER, RHIN, RUTA, UNIR

5 ALTAR, AVOIR, DRESS, ENTRO, EREDI, FALSO, IMMEM, ISOLA, LETTE, MOCHE, MOULE, ZEDER

6 ADEPTO, ADOPTÉ, LÉZARD, LUCIDE, LYZEUM, TRAEGE, TULIPE, UNIONE

7 ELETTRO, ÉLEVAGE, ENERGIE, ERIGERE, PALADIN, PALAZZO, TORCERE, UMFRAGE

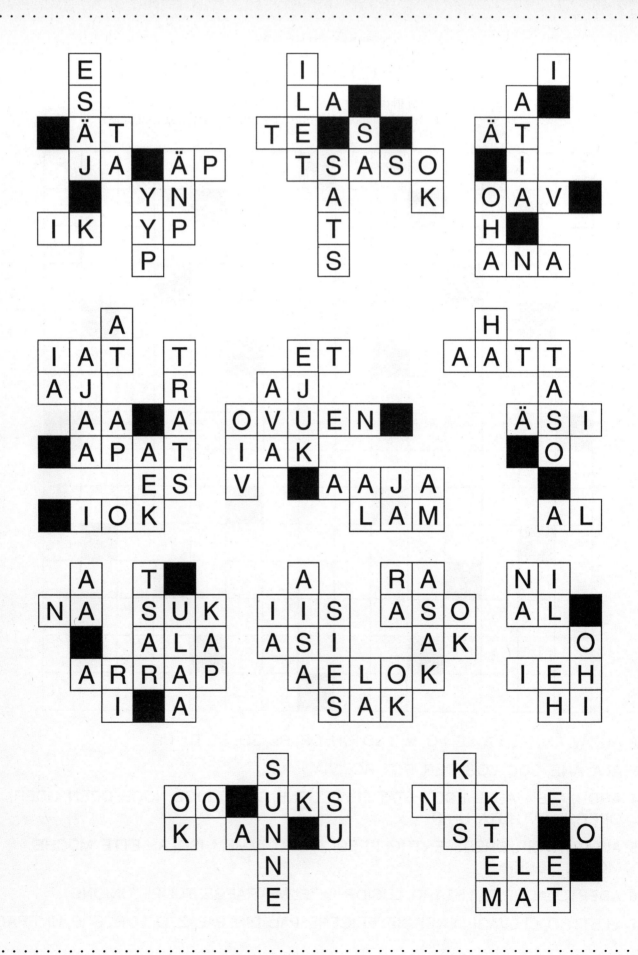

MOSAIC

Wherein the question becomes the answer.

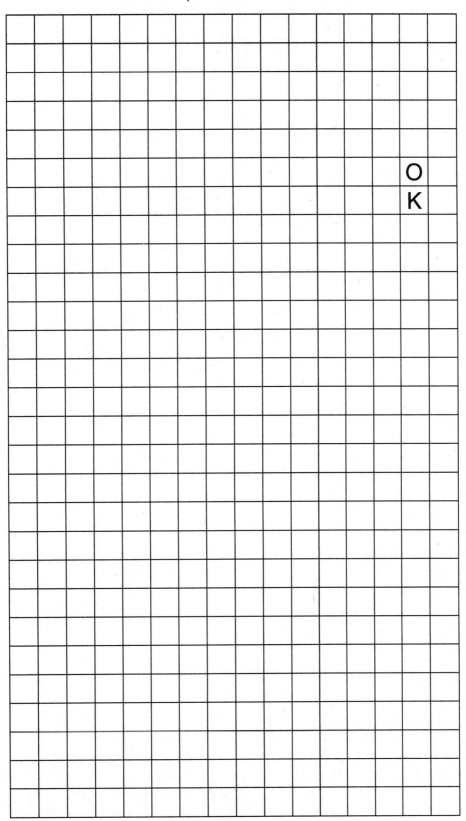

COMING OR GOING

Replace each letter in the diagram with the one which precedes OR follows it in the alphabet,
to get the names of the following celebrities (listed below in random order):

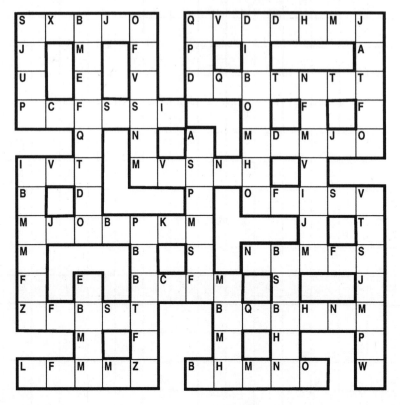

ACROSS

- French writer (Louis, 1897-1982)
- American statesman (Abraham, 1809-1865)
- Irish poet (William Butler, 1865-1939; Nobel)
- American writer (Mark, 1835-1910)
- Czech reformer (Jan, 1369-1415)
- German rocket builder originating from Romania (Hermann, 1894-1989)
- American dancer, actor and director (Gene, 1912-1996)
- Finnish Olympic athlete (Paavo, 1897-1973)
- Norwegian mathematician (Niels Hendrik, 1802-1829)
- Italian opera composer (Giacomo, 1858-1924)
- Dutch humanist (from Rotterdam, 1469?-1536)
- Israeli writer (Samuel Yosef, 1888-1980; Nobel)
- French painter (Edouard, 1832-1883)
- Soviet statesman (Vladimir Ilich, 1870-1924)
- Indian statesman (Jawaharlal, 1889-1964)

DOWN

- French physicist and astronomer (Dominique Frans, 1786-1853)
- English novelists (Anne, 1820-1849; Charlotte, 1816-1855; Emily Jane, 1818-1848)
- English physicist and mathematician (Sir Isaac, 1643-1727)
- English actor and writer (Peter, b. 1921)
- Norwegian dramatist (Henrik, 1828-1906)
- Yugoslav statesman (Josip Broz, 1892-1980)
- Danish narrative writer (Hans Christian, 1805-1875)
- English astronomer (Edmond, 1656-1742)
- American journalist and poet (Edgar Allan, 1809-1849)
- British film actor, director and producer (Sir Charles, 1889-1977)
- American violinist and conductor (Yehudi, b. 1916)
- Austrian opera composer (Leo, 1873-1925)
- Austro-American film director (Fritz, 1890-1976)
- Irish dramatist (Sean, 1880-1964)

LABYRINTH

Insert the words from the list below along the drawn paths, beginning with the marked squares (the numbers indicate the length of each word). The horizontal lines will reveal the names of great figures in culture and history.

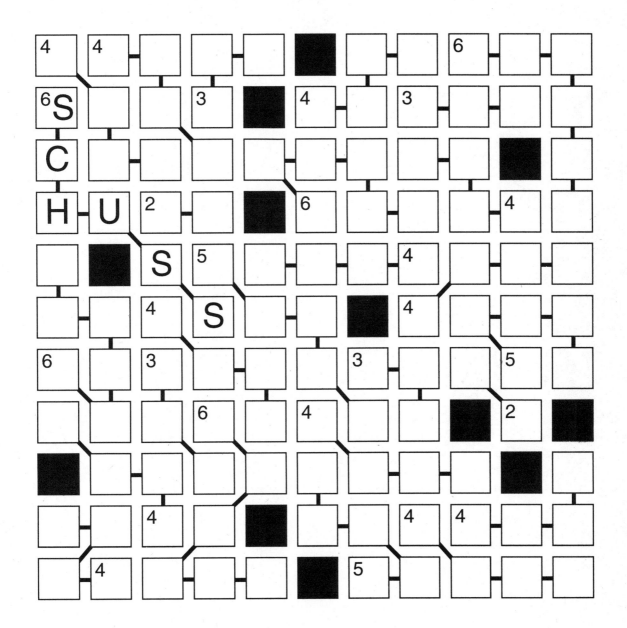

2 DA, GO

3 AHN, PER, WIE, ZAR

4 BERG, BLEI, CHOR, DIES, EDEL, EKEL, LEIN, MOOS, OHNE, REIN, URAN, WIND

5 PARSE, ROHRE, STADT

6 ISOMER, MANTEL, MEILEN, SCHACH, (SCHUSS)

ORDER, ORDER

Put the frames of the cartoon below in the correct logical order.

SOLUTION

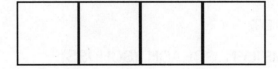

TURN, TURN, TURN

Draw a continuous, closed path running through every square exactly once without crossing itself, so that between two consecutive circles the line changes direction once if those circles are of different colors, but remains straight if the circles have the same color.
Transfer the resulting path into the letter matrix, mark the squares which contain direction changes, and copy them line by line beginning at the top. The letters you have copied will reveal the secondary solution of this puzzle.

Example:

Z	A	G	Y	Q	F	S	R
A	U	T	E	K	C	B	O
R	D	I	E	S	J	P	I
L	M	L	I	T	X	D	E
A	Z	U	X	P	B	B	U
E	U	H	R	Y	A	O	G
O	V	N	I	N	K	O	W
P	Z	W	V	I	U	L	A

BLOCK PARTY

From each numbered block draw one or more straight horizontal or vertical lines which pass through as many blocks altogether as indicated by the corresponding number. The numbered block itself is not counted. No lines intersect or overlap and no block remains empty.

Example:

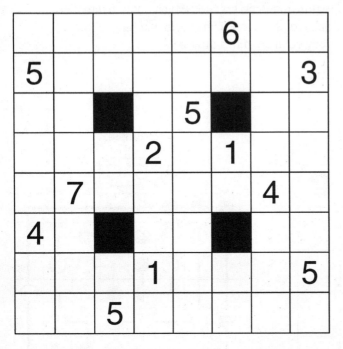

(IN-)EQUALITIES

Complete the puzzle diagram with numbers from 1 to 5 in such a manner that all given inequalities and equalities are simultaneously fulfilled.

LET'S GO TO THE MOVIES

Replace the numbers with letters in this simple subsitution code to give you the last names of 11 actors when reading across and the name of a winner of 6 Academy Awards reading down the central column. Each number represents a unique letter.

3	4	11	1	2	3	11
11	12	7	2	13	4	3
14	2	8	3	13	15	16
12	17	11	3	4	18	5
3	2	14	4	3	6	5
10	3	4	5	16	4	19
20	2	5	6	17	4	3
11	2	8	7	16	12	5
9	20	21	8	4	4	17
18	15	11	9	12	3	22
20	23	12	10	16	15	17

23

MARGINALLY ACCEPTABLE

A   B   C   D   E

2 CV, DA, DP, EE, EE, EE, EE, EH, EI, IV, NN, NN, NW, SI, SO, ST

3 BIS, GEN, IST, LEE, NOT, RES, ROT, SIE, TEE, TON, TOR, USO

4 GONG, GROB, KALK, KINO, KLAR, KOCH, NEST, PAGE, PLUS, RUIN, TEEN, TUCH

5 GABEN, GASSI, GEIGE, GELEE, GOTHA, GORGO, LEGAT, LEUTE

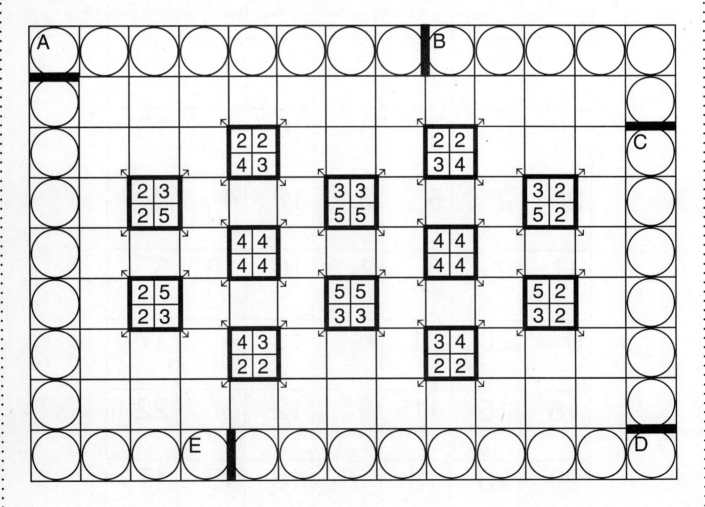

DRINKING SPREE

2	CE, ER, LT, UT
3	BAN, RAM, SPA
4	ARCH, IDEA, INNS, LUST
5	AGATE
6	HEARTY, SIESTA, THRILL
7	ARDUOUS, EPIGRAM, EUNUCHS
9	EMOTIONAL
10	IMMEMORIAL

2	AH, HE, LA, TA
3	APE, ROE, RUM, RUN, UGH
4	EMIT, LUMP, SNAG, TEAM
5	ASIAN, COLIC, SEAMS, TRIAL
6	CHESTY, LOOSEN
8	ADULATOR
10	HAMBURGERS, IDENTITIES

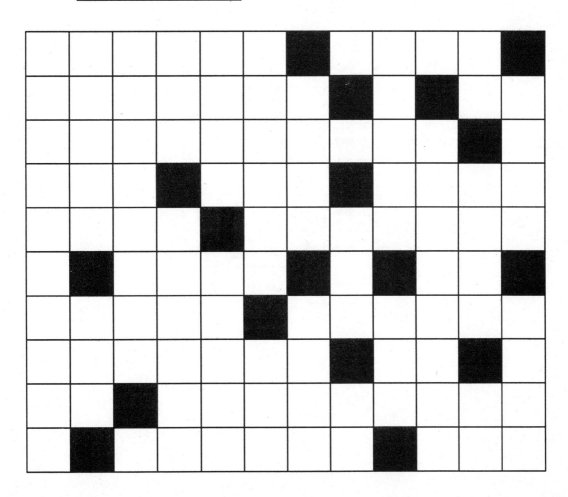

FOLLOWING DIRECTIONS

Find a path through the diagram, starting at S and ending at ★.
You may jump over squares, but may only land in each square once.

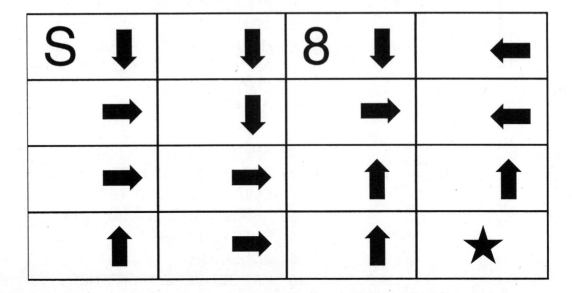

Example:

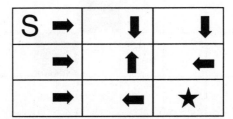

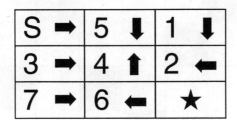

MEET YOU 'ROUND THE CORNER

Connect each X and O, so that –
• the connecting lines run only horizontally and vertically and each has one 90° turn
• every empty square has a line passing through it
• no lines intersect or overlap each other

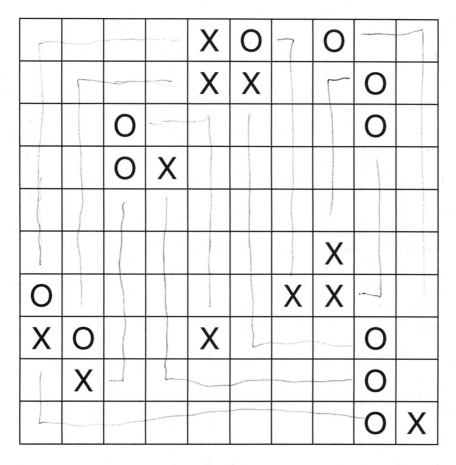

Example:

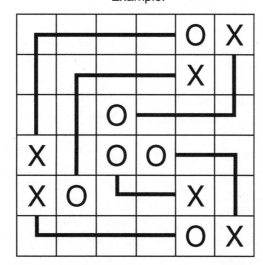

27

URBAN GRIDLOCK

The letters indicated in the column on the left must be placed to create a grid containing names
of important cities from the specified countries, plus the following two letter groups:
AF, AH, AR, AY, BR, BX, BY, DA, ED, EE, IA, IO, IR, JN, KM, KP, MN,
OI, ON, OS, PU, RE, RN, SA, SE, SI, SR, SS, TP, UX, YK, YW

1	2	3	4	5	6	7	8	9	10	11	12	13
2												
3												
4												
5												
6												
7												
8												
9												
10												
11												
12												

→ ACROSS

1	AADEIKOOPRSTT	– Japan, USA (Michigan)
2	ADEEEHMNNNOPP	– Yemen, Kampuchea
3	AAAAEHIIJKKRVY	– Iceland
4	AAEEIKMNRSSSW	– Great Britain (Wales)
5	ABMOORRRSSSST	– Bosnia and Hercegovina
6	AAAABIIMOPRRR	– Surinam
7	AAEEEINPSSSUZ	– Samoa, Egypt, Germany
8	AAAADKLLLSSTU	– Zambia, USA (Texas)
9	BCEEGIMNOO (=Ö) RYY	– Hungary
10	AAAADDKKMNRRS	– Uzbekistan
11	AAAAEFIILMNORU	– the Philippines, Russia (Bashkiristan)
12	ABBDEIMNNOORX	– Saudi Arabia, Czech Republic

↓ DOWN

1	AAEILMNOPPRRS	– France, Italy
2	AADDEEMOPSSU	– Ukraine, the Netherlands
3	ABBEEINRSSWY	– Australia
4	AAAAADIKNRSY	– Turkey
5	ACIJKKLMNOPS	– Russia, Colombia
6	AAAAAMMNNSSU	– Bahamas, Jordan
7	AADDEENORRRV	– Great Britain, Japan
8	AABEEGIIMMRZ	– USA (Florida), Croatia
9	BEKKKLOPTUXY	– Japan
10	ABEFILMOORSS	– France, Norway
11	AAAINNORRSST	– Italy
12	AADEHIINORRS	– Zimbabwe, Lebanon
13	AEEHIKNOORTT	– Iran, Japan

WRITERS BLOCK

Reconstruct in the diagram on the left a matrix of "hidden words", using the names of the following Nobel Prize winners for literature (to be inserted across, down or diagonally, forward or backword). The beginning of each word is marked by a white circle (o), the end by a black one (•).

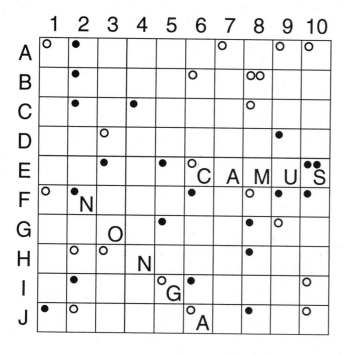

2 OE

4 GIDE, MANN, SHAW

5 (AGNON), (CAMUS), ELIOT, HESSE, HEYSE, SACHS, YEATS

6 ANDRIC, DUGARD, HAMSUN, JENSEN, ONEILL

7 LAXNESS, MISTRAL, ROLLAND

10 GALSWORTHY

When transferred into the diagram below, the squares remaining unused form the supplementary solution.

	1	2	3	4	5	6	7	8	9	10
A	C	K	S	A	J	M	D	K	V	S
B	R	D	I	O	T	X	I	W	E	U
C	F	X	I	H	F	B	Q	A	R	G
D	U	B	N	N	C	T	O	R	C	J
E	E	L	P	P	V	L	D	E	Z	Y
F	R	A	J	V	G	H	L	M	B	H
G	M	X	Q	I	O	F	W	Q	L	P
H	W	E	E	S	B	M	A	T	N	Z
I	H	C	Z	T	D	I	N	K	O	U
J	Y	O	F	A	U	S	G	P	G	Y

[ ][ ][ ][ ][ ][ ][ ][ ][ ][ ]

EDISON

Reassemble the mechanism!

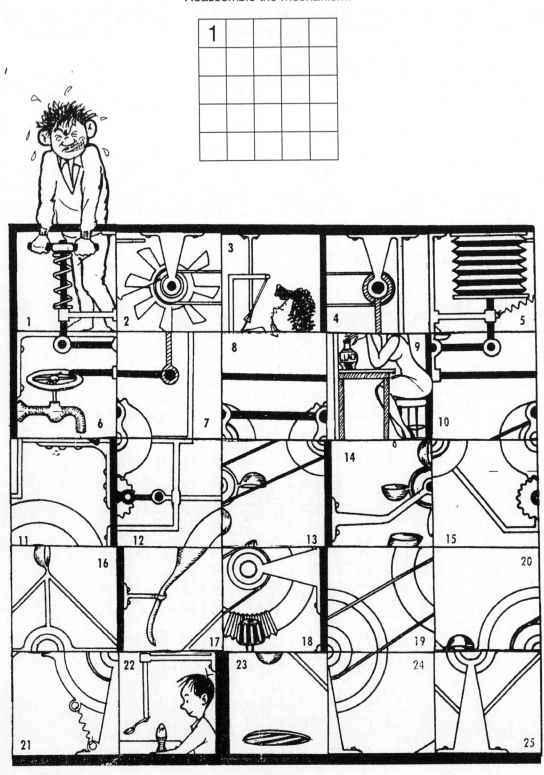

Form all possible two-digit combinations with the numbers 1, 2, 3, 4 (11, 12, 13, ..., 23, 24, 31, ..., 43, 44) and insert the missing ones in such a way that no digit appears twice in the same position in any row or column.

		12	
34			
	43		32

Example:

11	09	60	96
90	66	01	19
06	10	99	61
69	91	16	00

EASY AS . . .

Divide the diagram into seven sections each of which contains an A, a B, and a C.
The sections may have different shapes and sizes.

			A			
B	B				B	A
B			B	C		C
	B	C		A		C
	A		C	A		C	B
A	A			C		

31

WHO'S WHO

The following names (in random order) must be formed in the diagram using the given fragments.

A - A - A - A - A - D - E - E - E - E - G - H - H - I - I - I - K - K - L -
M - M - N - N - O - R - R - S - S - S - S - S - T - T - W
AR - DE - DE - ER - ER - HA - KE - KI - KI - LA - LI - LL - MA - ND - NG - NI -
ON - PE - PL - RA - SC - TE - TO - TZ - UE - ZO
ANT - ART - CHE - DAN - ELA - ERI - GOR - ING - PAD - PER - RER - TUR - USS - VEL

ACROSS
- English poet and dramatist (William, 1564-1616)
- Chinese imperial dynasty (1368-1644)
- French astronomer and physicist (Dominique François, 1786-1853)
- German philosopher (Friedrich, 1844-1900)
- The founder of the Ursuline nuns order (Merici)
- The emperor of Japan (b. 1933)
- German painter and graphic artist (Albrecht, 1471-1528)
- Russian prince from Novgorod (Svyatoslavich, 1150-1202)
- British philosopher and mathematician (Bertrand, 1872-1970)
- German astronomer (Johannes, 1571-1630)
- French philosopher (René, 1596-1650)
- North Korean statesman (Il Sung, 1912-1994)
- Dutch painter (Adriaen van de, 1636-1672)
- Argentinean statesman (Juan Domingo, 1895-1974)
- Scottish economist (John, 1671-1729)
- Irish dramatist (Richard Brinsley, 1751-1816)
- French writer (Emile, 1840-1902)
- German philosopher (Immanuel, 1724-1804)
- American silent film actor and director (Max, 1883-1925)
- German writer (Thomas, 1875-1955)

DOWN
- French actor (Alain, b.1935)
- French writer (Eugène, 1804-1857)
- Czech writer and statesman (Vaclav, b. 1936)
- Turkish statesman (1881-1938; 2 words)
- The Greek goddess of discord
- Italian poet (Alighieri, 1265-1321)
- American singer and actress (b. 1946)
- American statesman (Al(bert), b. 1945)
- American authoress (Marjorie Kinnan, 1896-1953)
- English writer (Rudyard, 1865-1936)
- South African statesman (Nelson, b. 1918)
- Italian conductor (Arturo, 1867-1957)
- Hungarian leader (d.907)
- German statesman (Theodor, 1884-1963)
- French philosopher and writer (Jean-Paul, 1905-1980)
- German statesman (Roman, b.1931)
- Viking seafarer (the Red, d.1007?)
- Japanese physicist (Leo., b.1925)

CRYPTO-CROSS-SUM

The letters and letter pairs written into the diagram represent numbers, each letter corresponding to the same number every time. Each of the numbers at the top of a column or left side of a row represents the sum of those figures between 1 and 9 which have been entered into the corresponding row or column. Within any of those areas you may not repeat any numbers.
Fill in the diagram so that both in the horizontal and in the vertical line the additions are correct.

	RY	RA	RI	YO		YN	RA	H	L
YO					RR				
AO			R		AY		Y		
	AO	RA/T			RI/T			L	AR
B		RH/AO				T/AI			
BN	L	A	B	Y	R	I	N	T	H
RY				RR	I / RA				
	N	RB/RR			N		B	RI	L
RT			N		AR				
RR	R				AI				

1	2	3	4	5	6	7	8	9	0

THIS:THAT

Two letter groups (in alphabetical order):
AC AL AO CE CI EA EM FC GK IM IS KF LA NL NR RA RI SI SM TL

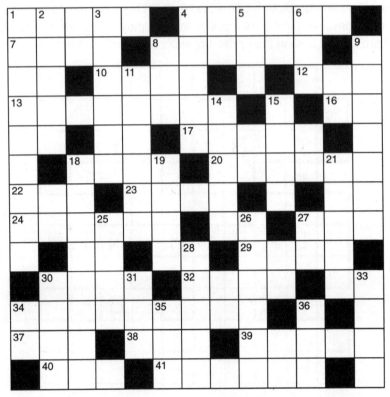

ACROSS

1 1972:SALT::1982:?
4 Egypt:Suez::Central America:?
7 Samuel Langhorne Clemens:Mark Twain::
Edson Arantes do Nascimento:?
8 6:"Pastorale"::3:"?"
10 aero:Delta. astro:?
12 nose:rhino::ear:?
13 the Himalayas:Yeti::South America:?
16 neon:Ne::lutetium:?
17 Paris:"César"::Hollywood:"?"
18 Boris:Becker::Steffi:?
20 Rome:Caesar::Tokyo:?
22 Bonn:Maastricht::DM:?
23 Augustus:Augusta::Divus:?
24 1989:Bush::1981:?
27 Washington:CIA::Moscow:?
29 USA 1994:England 1996::FIFA:?
30 pro:contra::exo:?
32 Bruxelles:EU::Geneva:?
34 N/S:Equator::E/W:?
37 Havel (CS):"Charta 77"::Michnik (PL):?
38 U:Volt::R:?
39 Milan, Ohio:Edison::Osaka:?
40 Maurice:Chevalier::Morris:?
41 Hera:Zeus::Isis:?

DOWN

1 Tom Jones:Fielding::Indiana Jones:?
2 Guglielmo:Marconi::Nikola:?
3 Kirk/Michael:Douglas::August/Jean:?
4 Paris:Louvre::Madrid:?
5 Romania:RO::Nicaragua:?
6 Europe:China::Marx:?
8 Apollo:Ariane::NASA:?
9 Ampere x volt:watt::ampere x second:?
11 1815 Wellington:Napoleon::1588 Francis Drake:?
14 Rome:Romulus::Turkey:?
15 Armenia:Yerevan::Azerbaijan:?
18 Beckenbauer:Matthäus::Stradivari:?
19 Tom:Huckleberry::Sawyer:?
21 Paul:Cezanne::Edgar:?
25 Nobel 1957:Camus::Nobel 1947:?
26 Geneva:Calvin::Wittenberg:?
28 Calvados:Caen::Champagne/Ardenne:?
30 Aurora:Eos::Cupid:?
31 John:Yoko::Lennon:?
33 Budapest:Danube::Frankfurt:?
35 Food and Agriculture Organization:FAO::World
Health Organization:?
36 Africa:OAU::America:?

A Capital Idea

Fill in the grid with the letters used so that each row, column and
3 x 3 square will contain each letter exactly once.

A			C		H			E
	H					S		
	C	T		R		B	H	
T			B			U		H
		C				E		
H			S		T			A
	B	U		H		A	E	
		E				T		
R				U		E		S

Example:

5	3	1	7	2	4	8	6	9
9	6	2	8	5	3	7	1	4
7	4	8	1	9	6	2	3	5
4	1	9	5	7	8	3	2	6
6	8	5	2	3	9	1	4	7
2	7	3	6	4	1	5	9	8
3	2	6	9	8	5	4	7	1
8	9	4	3	1	7	6	5	2
1	5	7	4	6	2	9	8	3

Reach For The Stars

Into each row and column insert as many stars as the numbers indicate.
Each arrow points in the direction of at least one star.
Note: No stars may touch each other horizontally or vertically.

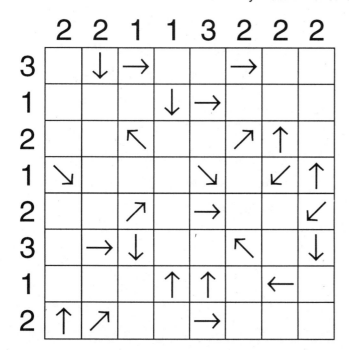

Example:

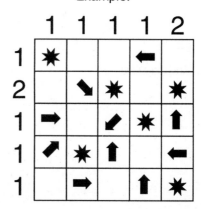

35

ALCHEMY

Insert the following words (across – Dutch, down – Spanish) into the grid
to reveal chemical compounds and – using the letters in the marked squares –
a fourth answer from a related family.

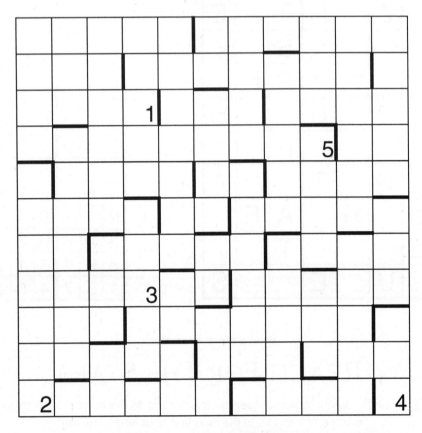

ACROSS

2 AL, EN, TE, UI

3 LES, OMA, TAP, VOS

4 ANTI, BOER, LOOS, NOTA, REIS, VAAG

5 ALGEN, AREND, BRAND, GAPER,
NOORS, SINAS

6 CLERUS, NEIGEN, RIMBOE, STRESS

7 NEUROSE, UNANIEM

9 GARNIZOEN

DOWN

2 DO, EM, EN, SU, UN

3 AMO, AVE, ESA, GEL, SIN

4 AZUL, CASO, CLIP, GONG, NEON

5 ALISO, ENANO, SEDES, SEGUN,
TEMER, TRAGO

6 INSANO, OBRERO, SENTIR

7 ALINEAR, ASENTAR, PATRONA,
REVISAR

CHECKMATE

Taking into account the indicated symbols to be found in one of the diagrams
(reconstructed by means of the Turkish words listed below)
you will discover a chess problem with white to move and checkmate in two moves.

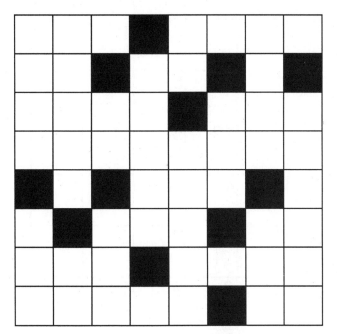

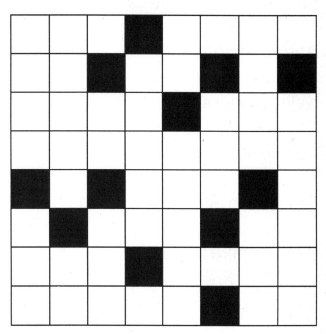

Ü   K   H   D   Ö

2 AD, AL, AN, AR, DA, KI, KA, NA, NE, OD, OF, SA, TA, TÜ, YA

3 AIT, AST, ATA, BEL, BRE, DUT, IKA, IKI, KAR, LIF, LIM, ÖRF, RET, TAT, UDI, ÜST, ÜTÜ, YAS

4 AHIT, AKÇA, BATI, ÇATI, EFOR, IKIZ, IMAL, IRAT, NEBI, ÖNEM

5 ALEYH, KIRAZ, OTARI, REFAH, REFÜJ, SALIH, TAMAH, TRETE

6 ARDALA, ÜZÜNTÜ

8 MÜFESSIR, ZARARSIZ

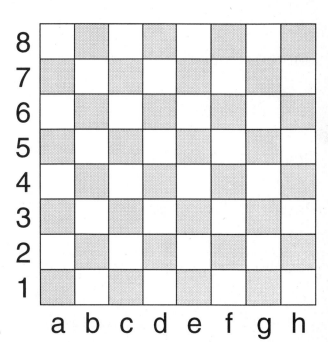

THREE ON A MATCH

Fahrenheit, Kelvin, ...

Angel, Victoria, ...

Kelly, Rogers, ...

Yoshihito, Hirohito, ...

Teheran, Yalta, ...

(H.) Lloyd, (B.) Keaton, ...

furioso, presto, ...

Seoul, Barcelona, ...

Petrosian, Spassky, ...

Catania, Messina, ...

Romeo, Ruslan, ...

Yale, Stanford, ...

New York, Brno, ...

Pavarotti, Carreras, ...

Vilnius, Riga, ...

1 C	2 E	3 L	4 S	5 I	6 U	4 S
7 N	5 I	8 A	9 G	8 A	10 R	8 A
8 A	4 S	11 T	8 A	5 I	10 R	2 E
8 A	19 R	5 I	12 H	5 I	11 T	13 O
14 P	13 O	11 T	4 S	15 D	8 A	16 M
1 C	12 H	8 A	14 (P)	3 L	5 I	7 N
8 A	3 L	3 L	2 (E)	9 G	10 R	13 O
8 A	11 T	3 L	8 (A)	7 N	11 T	8 A
17 F	5 I	4 S	1 (C)	12 H	2 E	10 R
14 P	8 A	3 L	2 (E)	10 R	16 M	13 O
11 T	10 R	5 I	4 S	11 T	8 A	7 N
12 H	8 A	10 R	18 V	8 A	10 R	15 D
1 C	13 O	3 L	13 O	9 G	7 N	2 E
15 D	13 O	16 M	5 I	7 N	9 G	13 O
11 T	8 A	3 L	3 L	5 I	7 N	7 N

(Each number always corresponds to the same letter.)

THE HEIGHT OF PUZZLING

Insert the binary numbers in the grid. The numbers in the margin show (in ascending order) the length of the numbers appearing in each row or column. The position of the unused squares will help you deduce Solution I while the contents of the columns helps determine Solution II.

3	1	2	3		4	2	4	1	4		
5	7	6	5	8	4	6	4	7	4	8	8

		4	6													T
		3	8													R
		2	9													U
		3	8													N
1	1	2	5													E
			11													M
		5	6													V
		1	10													O
		1	10													S

I												

II				

1 ...
2 00, 01, 10, 11
3 001, 010, 100, 101
4 0001, 0010, 0100, 0110, 1001, 1010, 1100
5 00000, 00010, 00100, 10010,
6 000000, 001000, 001010, 100000
7 0000000, 1001000
8 00010100, 00100010, 00100100, 10000010, 10001001
9 100010000
10 0100011100, 0110000100
11 01001000011

FIFTH
WORLD PUZZLE
CHAMPIONSHIP

Held in Utrecht, the Netherlands, the 5th World Puzzle Championship broke new ground in several areas. One of them was in the team competitions, which included a 3-D sculpture puzzle, a marathon game-puzzle round staged in conjunction with a national game convention and a real-life skyscraper problem solved with real wooden sckyscrapers.

The tournament also featured some classic World Puzzle Championship-style puzzles including battleships, minesweepers and domino problems as well as some future classics, invented or popularized by our Dutch hosts. These include one we call EASY AS . . . (p. 75) and various snake problems – such as NESSIE (p. 45) and SNAKE PIT (p. 78). But don't just take our word for it. Go ahead, solve 'em yourself. With so many styles to choose from, you'll have your own new favorites too.

MADE IN THE SHADE

The number in each square indicates how many of the bordering squares should be shaded. Squares diagonally adjacent are also included. If a square contains a 0, then all of the bordering squares remain white. However, the square with the 0 itself can be shaded.

0	1	2	3	3	2	1
1	2	2	2	2	1	1
1	2	5	5	4	2	1
2	3	3	1	1	0	0
1	2	5	5	4	2	1
1	2	2	2	2	1	1
1	3	5	6	6	4	2
2	2	4	3	4	2	2
3	3	6	3	6	3	3
2	1	3	1	3	1	2
2	3	4	3	4	3	2
2	2	3	2	2	1	1
3	3	5	3	3	2	1
2	1	2	0	0	0	0
2	3	4	3	3	2	1
2	2	3	2	3	2	2
3	3	5	3	5	3	3
2	1	2	0	2	1	2
2	3	4	3	4	3	2
2	2	3	2	3	2	2
3	4	7	6	7	4	3
2	2	3	2	3	2	2
2	4	6	6	6	4	2
1	1	2	2	3	2	2
2	4	6	6	7	4	3
1	1	2	2	4	3	3
2	4	6	6	7	4	3
1	1	2	2	3	2	2
2	4	6	6	6	4	2
2	2	4	3	4	2	2
3	3	6	3	6	3	3
2	1	3	1	3	1	2
1	1	1	0	1	1	1

OUT OF AFRICA

Travel from Casablanca to Cape Town and make sure you pass checkpoints 1 to 8 on the way.
The checkpoints should be passed in the order 1 to 8 and each no more than once.
Roads and crossroads can be used only once. What is the **shortest** route?

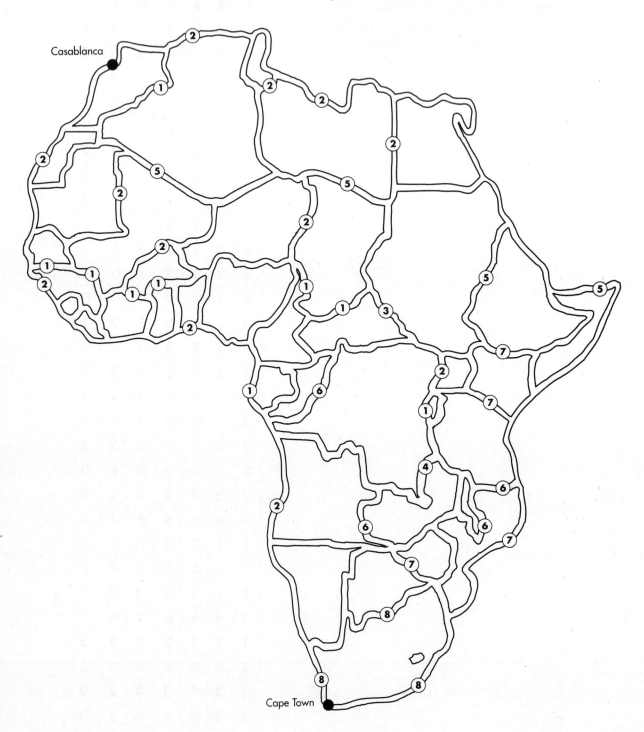

CAN YOU DIGIT?

The diagram below shows only parts of the digits involved in a subtraction problem.
They are composed according to the model shown. Can you reconstruct the calculation?

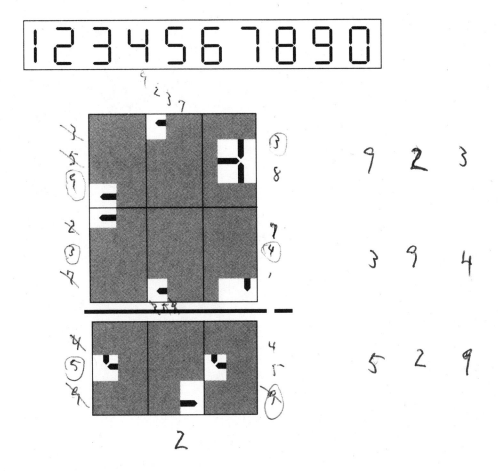

9 2 3

3 9 4

5 2 9

FRUIT SALAD

All fruit combinations indicated are represented in the diagram, and may occur in any direction.
Individual pieces of fruit may occur in more than one combination in the diagram.
Cross out all the combinations. How many apples are left?

44

NESSIE

A sea serpent, 45 meters long, not including its head and tail, lies under the surface of the water. The animal is bent horizontally and vertically, but doesn't touch itself anywhere, not even diagonally. Its head and tail are visible, as well as one other part of its body. The figures outside the diagram indicate how many parts of the snake can be found in each row or column. The black squares are rocks where the animal can't be. Can you establish its exact position?

BUILDING BLOCKS

Which two pairs can be used to form the two cubes? Pieces may be turned but not mirrored.

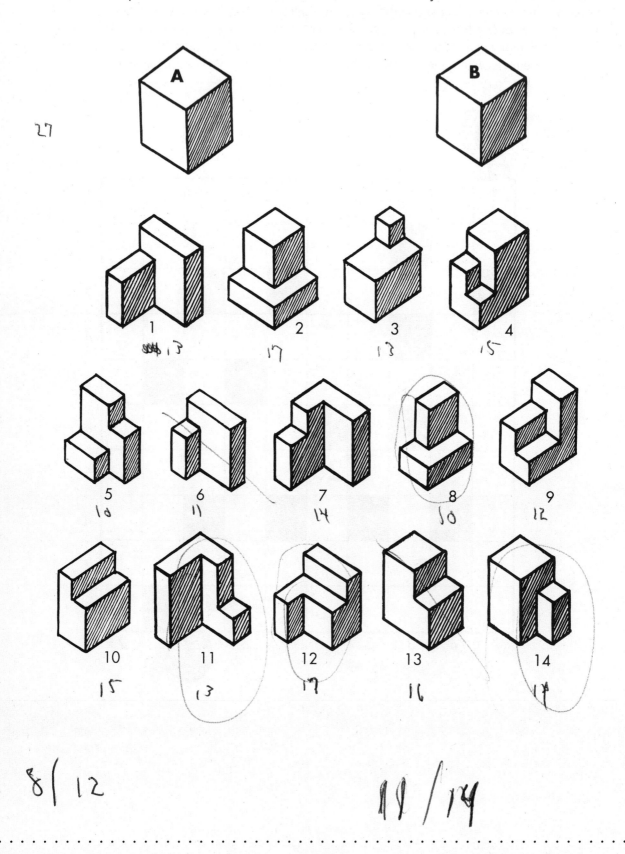

27

A   B

1   2   3   4

24, 13   17   13   15

5   6   7   8   9

18   11   14   10   12

10   11   12   13   14

15   13   17   16   17

8 / 12   11 / 14

FIGURE TREE

Fill in the figures 1 to 14 in such a way that the figure in each circle is equal to the sum of the figures in the circles into which it branches off. Example: the four circles into which the trunk branches off should contain figures that add up to a total of 44. Three figures have already been filled in.

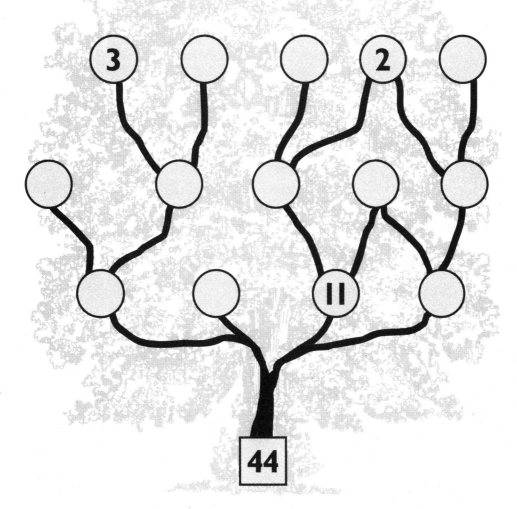

DOMINO THEORY

We have placed a complete set of 28 dominoes in the diagram below. However, the sides of the dominoes have been removed and the spots have been replaced by numbers. Can you draw the sides in the diagram so that it becomes clear exactly how the dominoes are positioned?

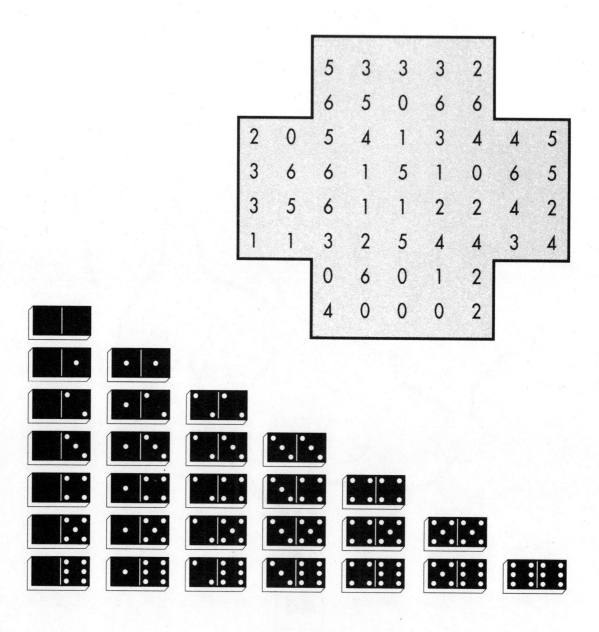

PENTOMINOS

Place the pieces inside the diagram in such a way that they don't touch each other anywhere, not even diagonally. Individual pieces may be turned but not mirrored. The numbers outside the diagram indicate how many parts of the pieces each row or column contains.

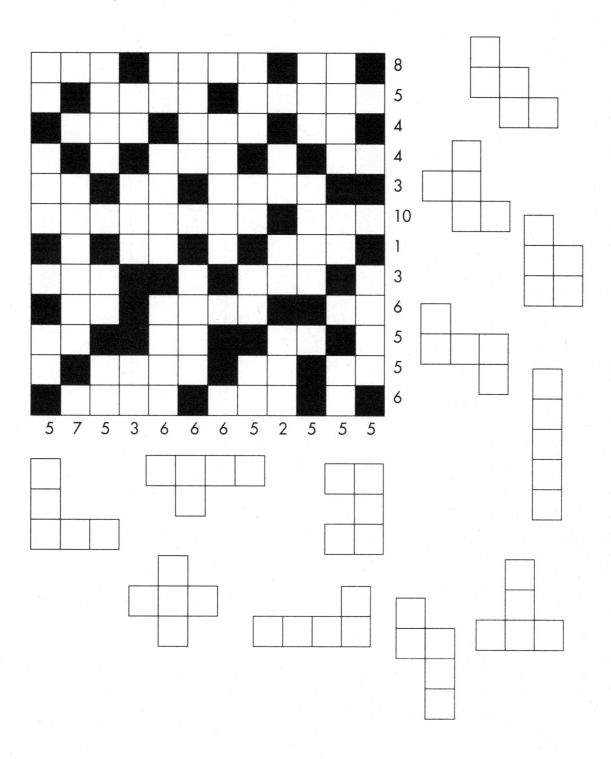

VANTAGE POINTS

Here you see the center of a small town. It is possible to station four police officers in such a way that they can keep an eye on all the streets just by turning around. Do you know where they are stationed?

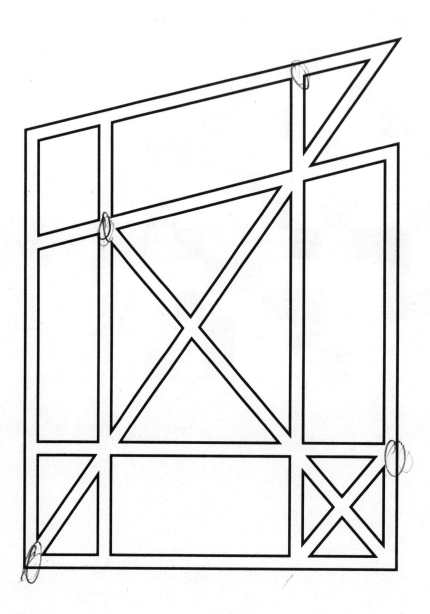

POLITICAL ASYLUM

The names of a number of presidents and heads of government are hidden in the diagram. There is no more and no less than one name in anagram form in each row and each column. All the letters in the diagram are used only once. Ö should be read as O. Once you have the correct solution, you will discover the name of another expert in the area of politics.

ARAFAT (Palestine National Authority)
ASSAD (Syria)
AZNAR (Spain)
BIYA (Cameroon)
BRUTON (Ireland)
CASTRO (Cuba)
CHIRAC (France)
GÖNCZ (Hungary)
HAVEL (Czech Republic)
KOHL (Germany)
KOK (The Netherlands)

KOVAC (Slovakia)
KUCAN (Slovenia)
LILIC (Yugoslavia)
MAJOR (Great Brittain)
MEKSI (Albania)
MENEM (Argentina)
MOI (Kenya)
PRODI (Italy)
REINA (Honduras)
SOARES (Portugal)
ZHELEV (Bulgaria)

H	S	I	L	I	T	O	M	I	K	S
Z	R	A	J	C	N	N	C	R	O	G
A	A	R	A	N	C	E	I	E	I	S
R	A	L	I	O	U	M	A	H	M	E
V	I	E	R	K	B	H	R	L	B	A
N	O	E	V	A	Z	L	E	D	H	R
A	A	C	U	S	N	C	H	N	K	V
T	F	A	E	A	A	M	C	P	A	R
Z	C	O	M	E	O	E	K	K	L	A
L	T	L	S	D	A	A	I	O	S	O
C	O	I	O	M	R	I	V	A	Y	K

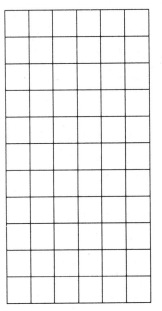

VALUE ADDED

Each of the rectangles has a value between 1 and 9. Each value occurs only once. When two or more rectangles overlap, their values are added. We have indicated some of these sums in the diagram. What are the values of rectangles A to I?

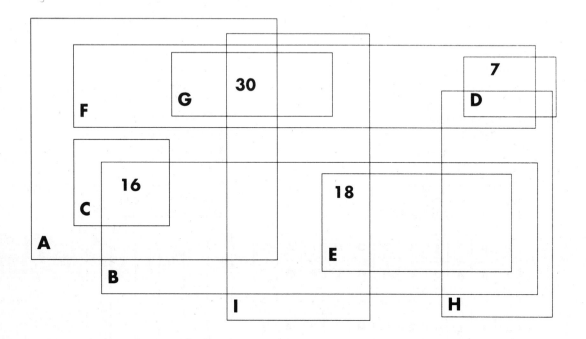

A	B	C	D	E	F	G	H	I

SYMBOLISM

Each letter always represents the same digit. Find out what the digits are.

$$A\ B\ C\ B\quad -\quad D\ E\ F\ C\quad =\quad G\ A\ F\ B$$

$$\div\qquad\qquad +\qquad\qquad -$$

$$D\ H\quad \times\quad A\ B\quad =\quad I\ E\ I$$

$$=\qquad\qquad =\qquad\qquad =$$

$$G\ G\ E\quad +\quad D\ E\ B\ B\quad =\quad D\ H\ D\ G$$

A	B	C	D	E	F	G	H	I

JIGSAW LETTERS

Place the "words" in the diagram.

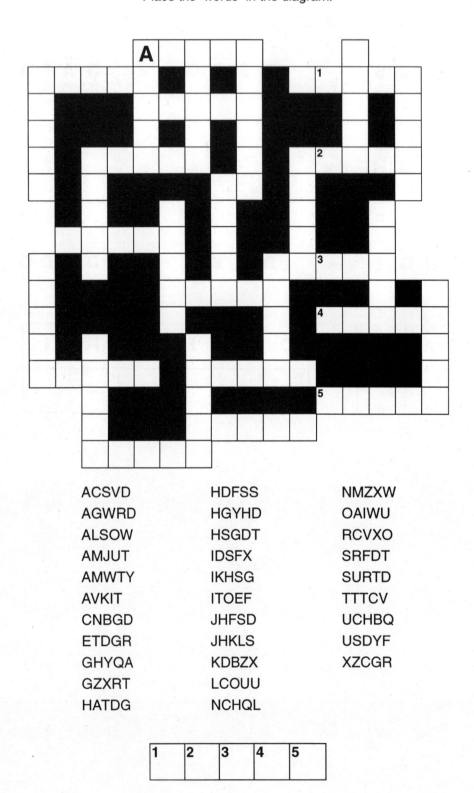

ACSVD	HDFSS	NMZXW
AGWRD	HGYHD	OAIWU
ALSOW	HSGDT	RCVXO
AMJUT	IDSFX	SRFDT
AMWTY	IKHSG	SURTD
AVKIT	ITOEF	TTTCV
CNBGD	JHFSD	UCHBQ
ETDGR	JHKLS	USDYF
GHYQA	KDBZX	XZCGR
GZXRT	LCOUU	
HATDG	NCHQL	

1	2	3	4	5

WEATHER WATCH

The meteorologist's screen below shows the position of a number of rainstorms.
All the storms are rectangular or square and at least two cells wide and two cells long.
The rainstorms don't touch each other anywhere, not even diagonally. The numbers outside
the diagram indicate how many parts of the storms can be found in each row or column.
What is the current position of the storms?

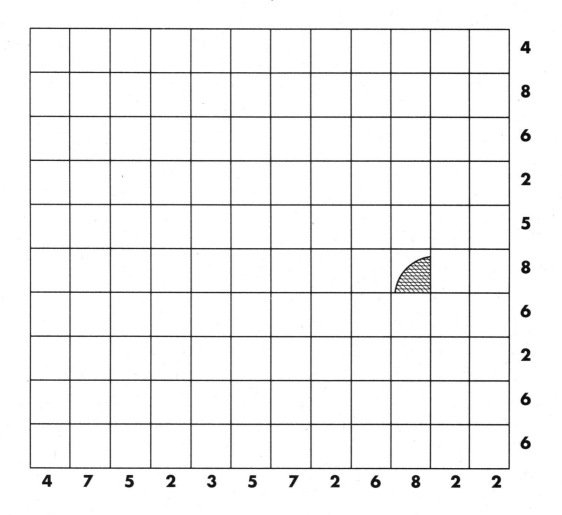

FIGURE FINDER

Locate the figures listed and cross them out in the figure field. They occur in any direction. There is a snag, though; if a slot is used for more than one figure, its value indicates the sum of the digits in that particular slot. What three digits are left in the figure field?

2	9	1	2	7	8	9	6
9	9	9	5	6	5	3	9
5	4	7	9	9	5	4	5
6	6	8	5	9	5	5	5
6	1	2	3	8	2	5	0
4	7	3	2	1	1	8	2
3	2	5	2	7	4	2	8
1	6	6	5	4	2	6	8

103335	362154	820555
211143	431025	821317
243517	458324	899126
255130	462572	987211
260541	624566	

PILLBOX

The figures 1 to 10 should be placed in ten of the twelve shaded shapes in the diagram. Each figure occurs only once. Two shapes contain no figure. The figures outside the diagram indicate the sum of the figures in the relevant row or column. Can you number the pillboxes?

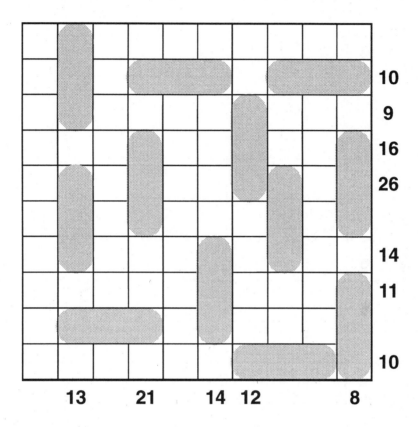

MINESWEEPER

There are exactly 35 mines hidden the diagram. The figures in the diagram indicate the number of mines that can be found in the squares immediately adjacent to that figure – horizontally, vertically or diagonally. There is a maximum of one mine per square. Squares with a figure do not contain mines.

	2	2	2	2	2	2		3	✗	✗	✗
										1	✗
1		3		2			3		2		
				2						3	
	4	∘	3			5		2	1		
1	4	∘								4	
	3	∘		2		1		3			
					3						2
2		3		2			3		2	✗	✗
					2		4		2		1
	1		1	1							1

BUILDING BLOCKS (PART II)

Place the sixteen blocks in the diagram in such a way that they produce correct equations from left to right and from top to bottom. The black cells mark the end of each equation. Disconnected figures or symbols do not occur. The + and − symbols only occur as part of a calculation. Where more than one calculation has to be carried out, multiplications are to be done before additions and subtractions.

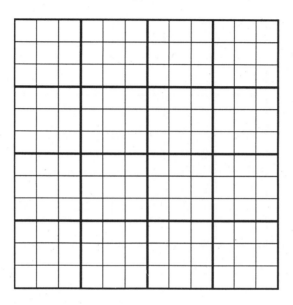

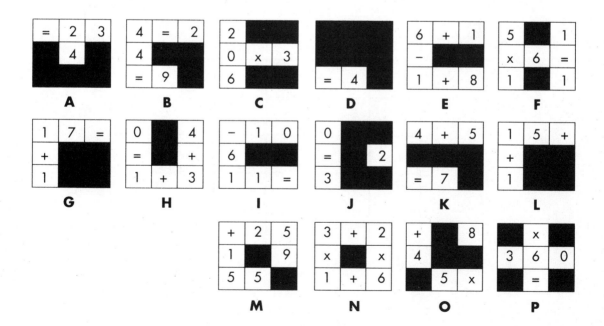

A   B   C   D   E   F

G   H   I   J   K   L

M   N   O   P

NUMBER GRID

Fill 12 different numbers into the diagram, such that there are two numbers in each row and two in each column. The numbers outside the diagram are the products of the two numbers in each row or column.

A

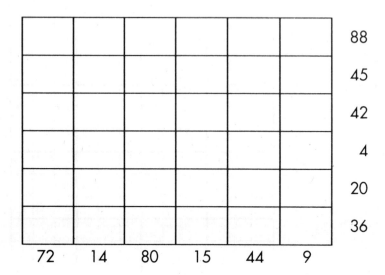

B

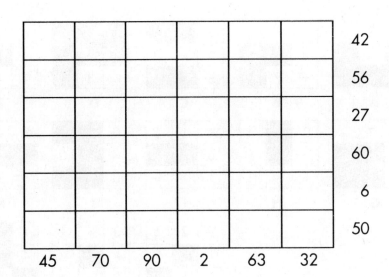

C

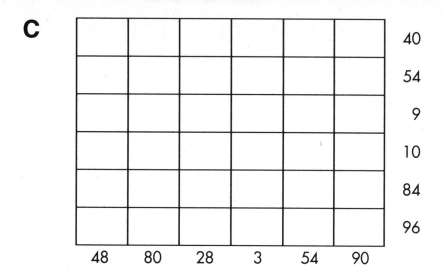

						40
						54
						9
						10
						84
						96
48	80	28	3	54	90	

D

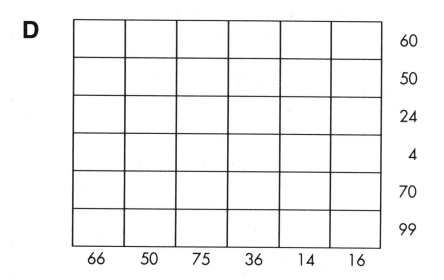

						60
						50
						24
						4
						70
						99
66	50	75	36	14	16	

E

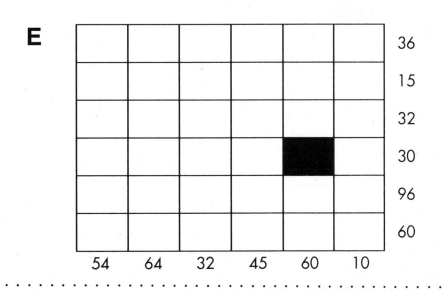

						36
						15
						32
						30
						96
						60
54	64	32	45	60	10	

CANALSIDE HOUSES

Below are the façades of ten typical houses by the Amsterdam canals.
There are a number of blocks next to each house. How do they fit
into the walls? You may turn the blocks but not mirror them.

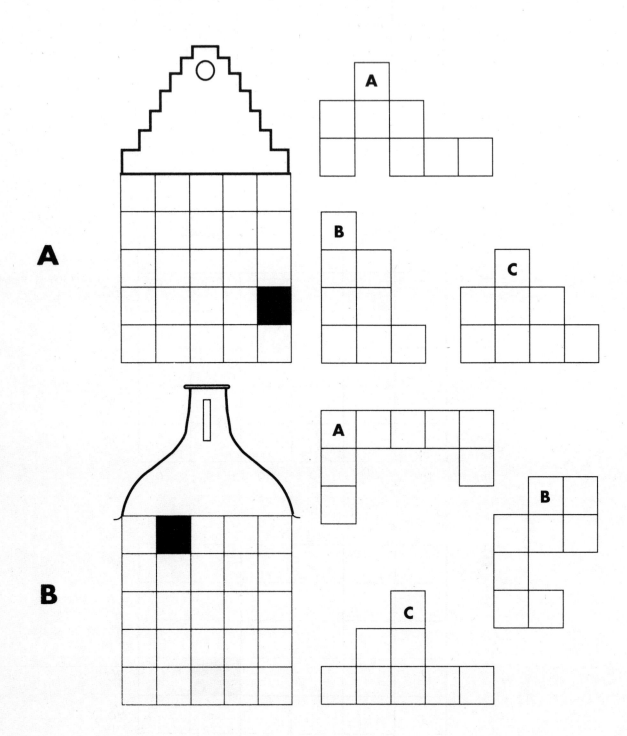

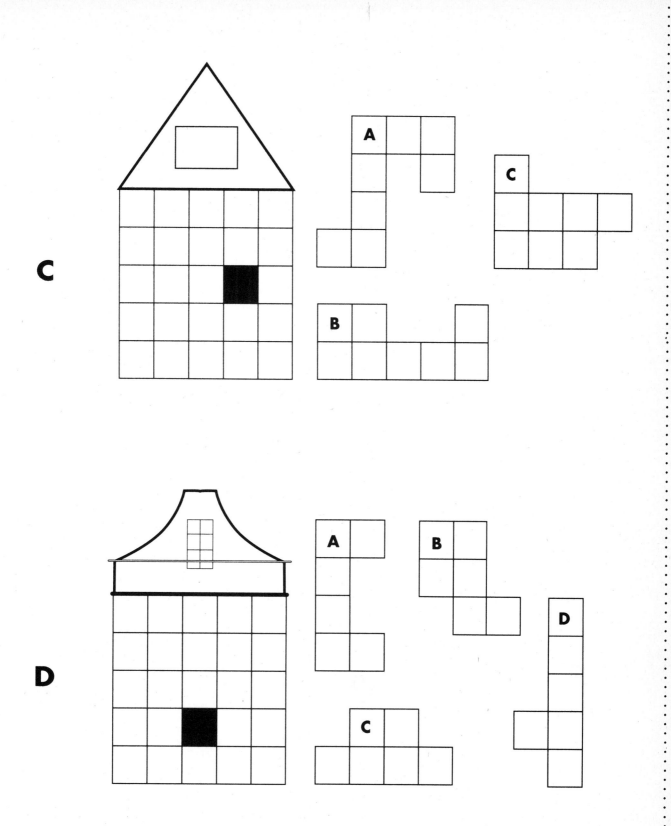

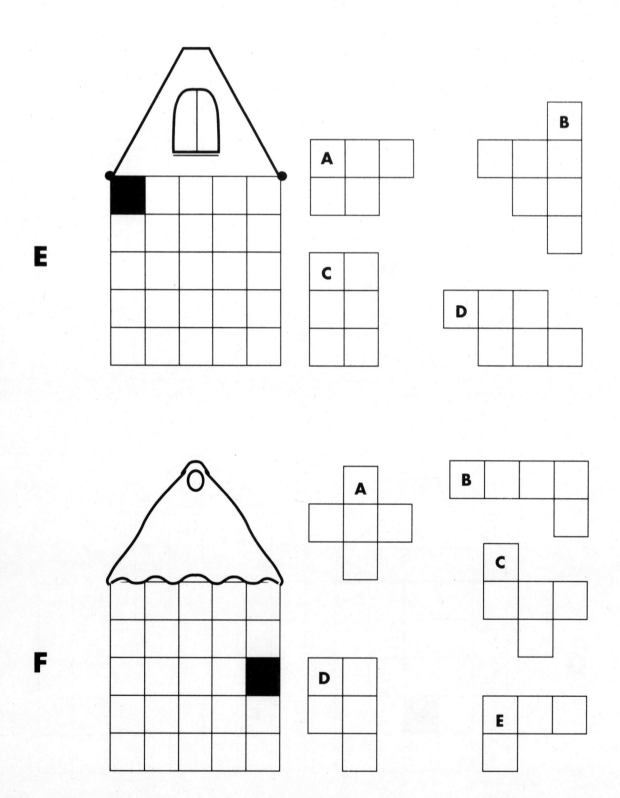

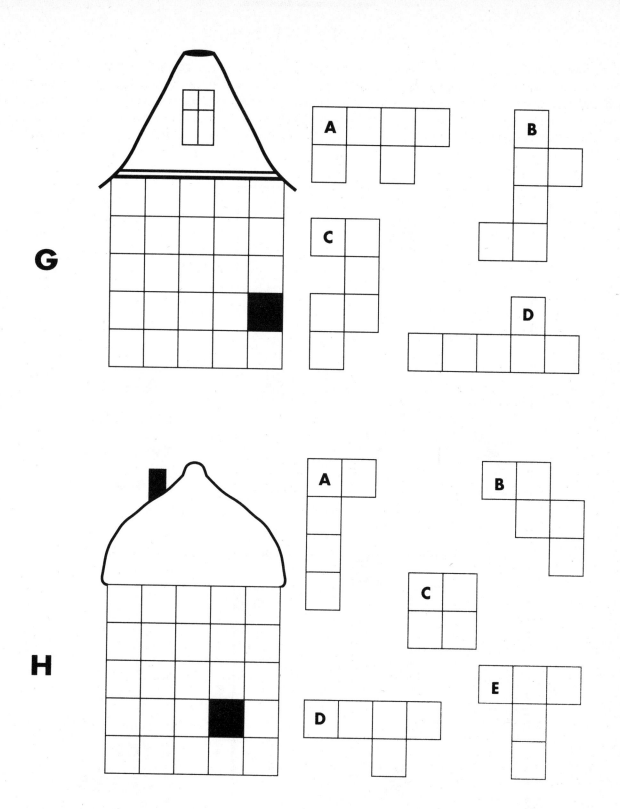

BATTLESHIPS

A number of hits have been filled in already in the diagrams below. As you can see from the fleets beside the diagram, you can work out some information about the position of the vessels by looking at the shape of these hits. Ships can be lying horizontally or vertically, and must not touch, not even diagonally. Squares marked with waves must remain empty. The numbers at the side and along the bottom of the diagram tell you how many parts of the vessels can be found in each row or column. Can you work out the position of these fleets?

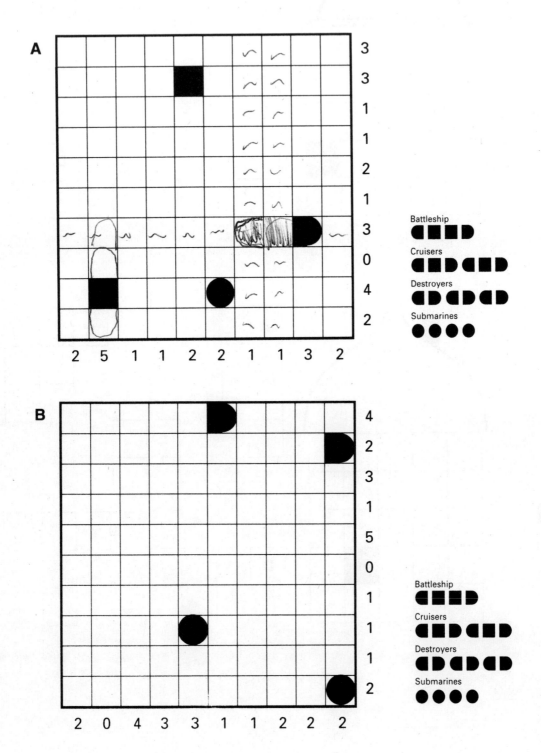

C

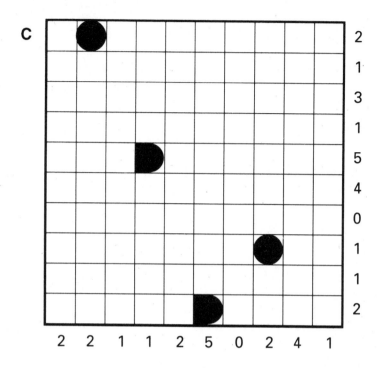

Right side values (top to bottom): 2, 1, 3, 1, 5, 4, 0, 1, 1, 2

Bottom values (left to right): 2, 2, 1, 1, 2, 5, 0, 2, 4, 1

Battleship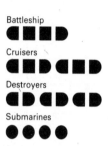

Cruisers

Destroyers

Submarines

D

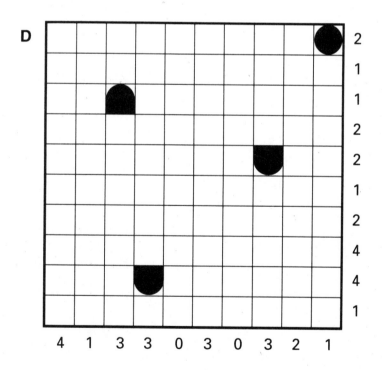

Right side values (top to bottom): 2, 1, 1, 2, 2, 1, 2, 4, 4, 1

Bottom values (left to right): 4, 1, 3, 3, 0, 3, 0, 3, 2, 1

Battleship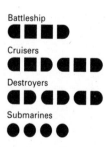

Cruisers

Destroyers

Submarines

E

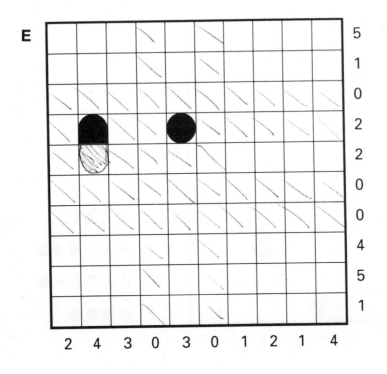

Grid E row clues (top to bottom): 5, 1, 0, 2, 2, 0, 0, 4, 5, 1

Grid E column clues (left to right): 2, 4, 3, 0, 3, 0, 1, 2, 1, 4

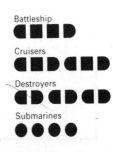

Battleship

Cruisers

Destroyers

Submarines

F

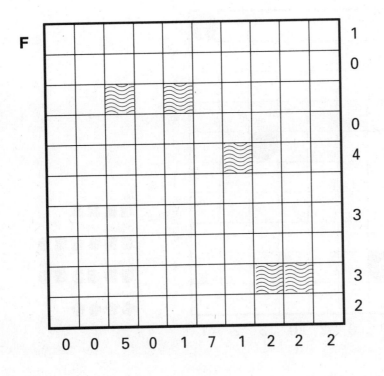

Grid F row clues (top to bottom): 1, 0, 0, 4, 3, 3, 2

Grid F column clues (left to right): 0, 0, 5, 0, 1, 7, 1, 2, 2, 2

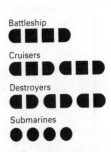

Battleship

Cruisers

Destroyers

Submarines

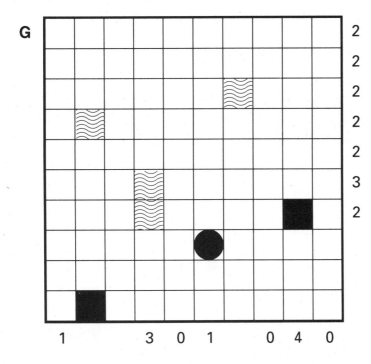

G

Row clues (top to bottom): 2, 2, 2, 2, 2, 3, 2

Column clues (left to right): 1, 3, 0, 1, 0, 4, 0

Battleship
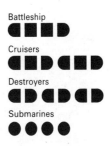

Cruisers

Destroyers

Submarines

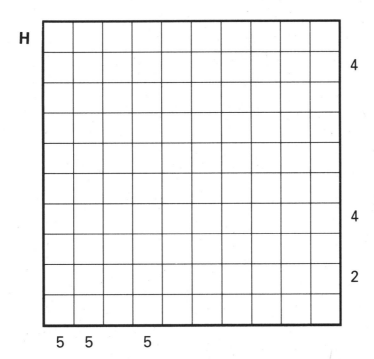

H

Row clues: 4, 4, 2

Column clues: 5, 5, 5

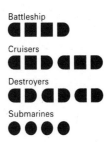

Battleship

Cruisers

Destroyers

Submarines

CROSS SUMS

The sum of the digits of each number to be filled in is equal to the figure in the black cell.
A figure above a diagonal refers to the digits to be filled in to the right of that cell.
A figure under a diagonal is the sum of the digits to be filled in under that specific cell.
The '0' is not used and a digit can never occur more than once in any sum.

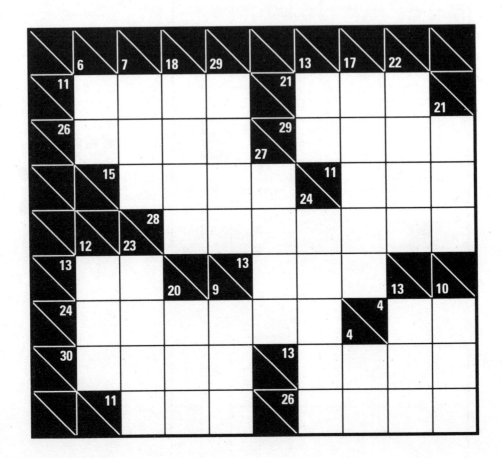

ONE-WAY TRAFFIC

We have indicated the positions of three parking spaces (indicated by the letter P) and seven shops (the black squares) on the map of this small town center. Some of the streets only allow one-way traffic; arrows indicate the direction of traffic, which is valid up to the first side street. Can you find a route that begins at one of the parking spaces, passes all the shops and ends at another parking space? Make sure that you don't have to visit any point on your route more than once.

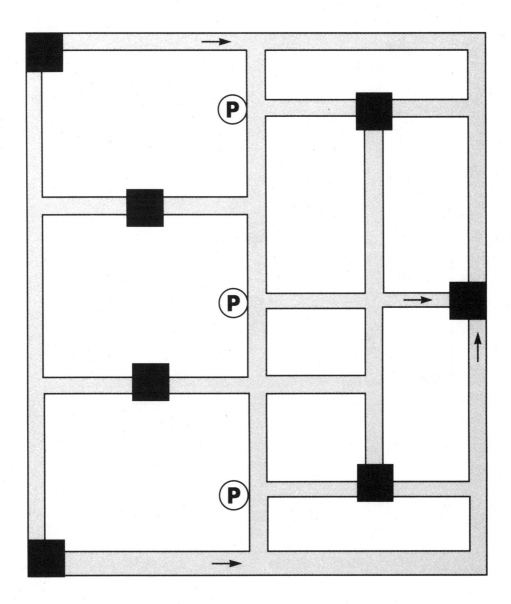

THE BEST SITES

Each guest at this campsite has his own tree. That means that each tent is placed directly next to, under or above the private tree, but not diagonally. The tents cannot be placed on adjoining sites, not even diagonally. The other day the campsite was fully booked. The figures outside the diagram indicate the number of tents that could be found in each row or column. Locate the sites of all the tents. One has already been given.

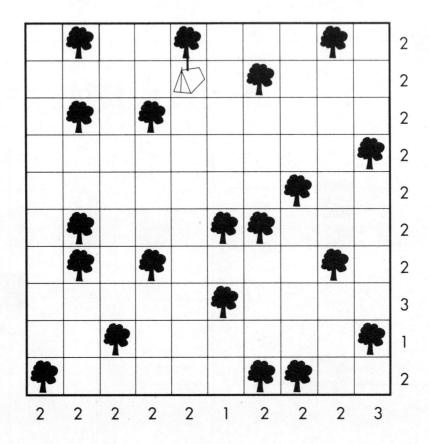

WORDS ACROSS SOUTH AMERICA

The list below contains the names of twelve South American countries and their capital cities.
Fill them into the diagram. The diagram already contains one letter from each name,
which is used for that name only. Every name crosses with one or more other names.

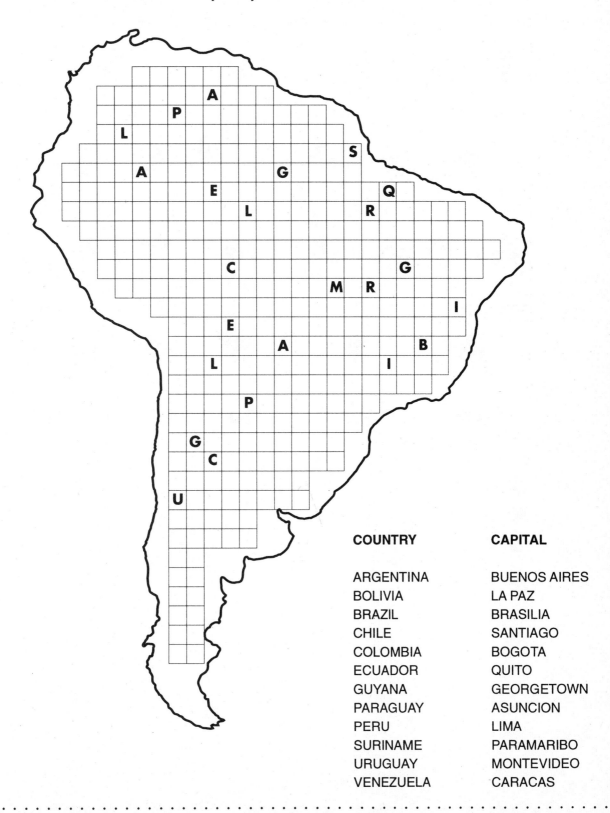

COUNTRY	CAPITAL
ARGENTINA	BUENOS AIRES
BOLIVIA	LA PAZ
BRAZIL	BRASILIA
CHILE	SANTIAGO
COLOMBIA	BOGOTA
ECUADOR	QUITO
GUYANA	GEORGETOWN
PARAGUAY	ASUNCION
PERU	LIMA
SURINAME	PARAMARIBO
URUGUAY	MONTEVIDEO
VENEZUELA	CARACAS

SUMS OF SYMBOLS

What is the value of each of the symbols below? The figures outside the diagram indicate the sum of all the symbols in each row or column.

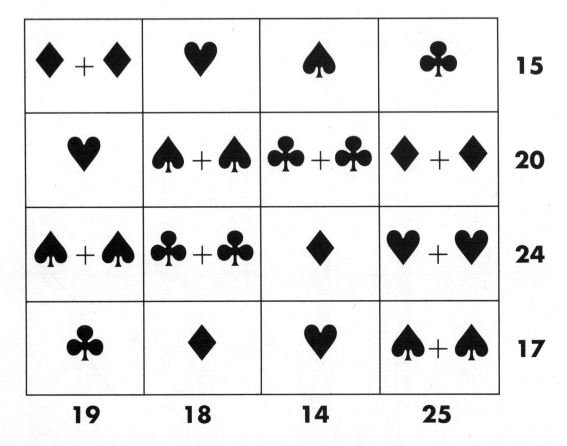

Fill in:

♠ =

♥ =

♦ =

♣ =

EASY AS . . . (PART II)

Try to fill in the letters A, B, C and D, each letter once, in each of the rows and columns. Twelve cells will remain empty. The letters outside the diagram are the letters you come across first from that direction.

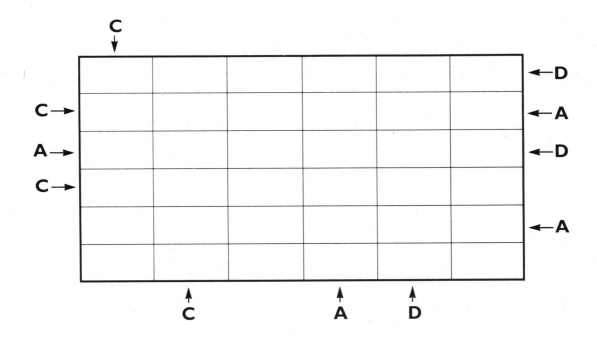

ANY WAY YOU CAN

Fill the Icelandic words from the list into the grid. The words may be placed from left to right, from right to left, from top to bottom and from bottom to top.

AFORM
AHUGI
ASAMT
BAKKI
DANSA
DEILA
DRAGA
GRATA
HVILA
KAFFI
KALDI
KERTI
KRAGI
~~NEFND~~
OPINN
SAMAN
STUND
SUMAR
TASKA
TOMUR
VINNA

CIRCLES AND SQUARES

Provide each empty cell with a figure from 1 to 10. The figures in the squares are equal to the sum of the figures in the adjoining circles. You don't have to use all the figures, and individual figures may be used more than once.

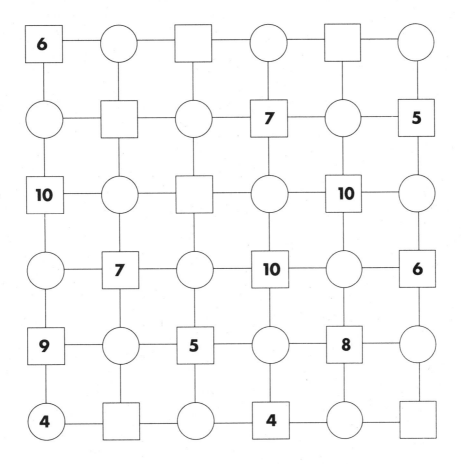

SNAKE PIT

Two snakes are hidden in the diagram. Each consists of pieces that are connected horizontally or vertically. Each snake may touch itself, but it cannot cross itself. The snakes do not touch each other, not even diagonally. The figures in the cells indicate how many pieces of one of the snakes adjoin the relevant cell horizontally, vertically or diagonally; the snakes cannot occupy the numbered cells.
The heads and tails of the two snakes are indicated with asterisks.

		*		2		*							
	2							4		7		5	2
			7			5							
3						6							
				3						0			
			2									6	
							0						
		5							4			6	
5					4				4				
	4					5	2				1		
		0											4
				4							5		
								2					*
	2			4					*				2

78

E-MAIL

These Italian words from the list all fit in the grid. All the Es have been filled in. But be careful: an E can also be a black square.

						E	E		E
E			E	E				E	E
			E	E		E			
	E	E		E			E		E
	E	E			E	E	E	E	E
	E				E			E	
E		E				E		E	
E		E	E		E			E	E
			E	E		E	E		
	E	E	E		E			E	E

2	3	4	5	7
IO	ALA	AREA	ESITO	CANZONE
MA	DEA	ARTE	OLTRE	CESSARE
ME	EST	ELLA	POETA	ESTERNO
NE	MAI	ENTE	PONTE	RENDERE
NO	NOI	EROE	REALE	ZELANTE
RE	ORA	PEPE	RESTO	
SE	OVE	VELA	STARE	
SI	PER		STILE	
TE			TERME	
			TORRE	

OUT OF AFRICA (PART II)

Travel from Cape Town to Casablanca via the shortest route and collect exactly 180 points on the way. You cannot use any road or crossroad more than once.

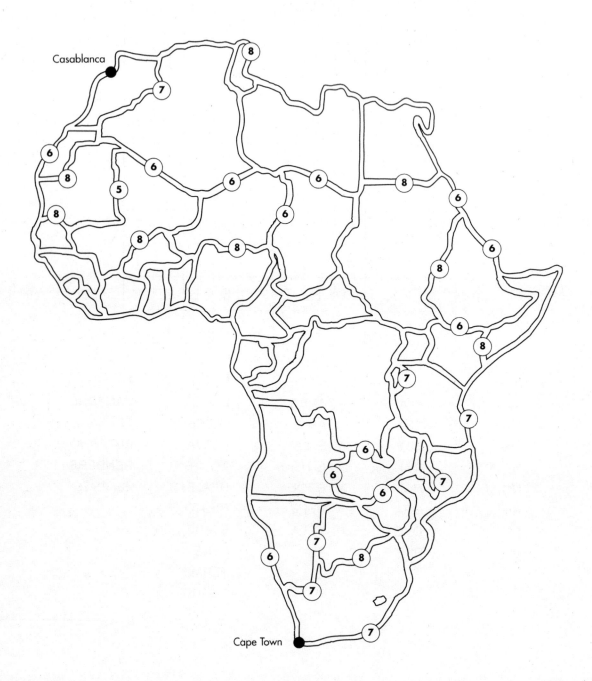

FIGURE SQUARE

Place the figures 1 to 6 in each of the rows and columns,
as well as in the two diagonals.

2			1		
					4
	2				
				6	
		5			1
3					

PUT THE PICTURES IN THE RIGHT ORDER

It seems like you never have time to stop.
Why should your airline?

Fly from Newark to Munich nonstop.

Now, Lufthansa offers you nonstop service from Newark to Munich with excellent connections to many major European cities. Experience the convenience of a nonstop, together with the renowned service and comforts you expect from Lufthansa.

 Lufthansa

TIMES BOOKS CROSSWORD ORDER FORM

VOL	ISBN	QUANTITY	PRICE	TOTAL PRICE

Random House Masterpiece Crosswords
Elegant, all-new crosswords plus profiles of famous puzzlemakers in a hardcover-spiral format.

VOL	ISBN	QUANTITY	PRICE	TOTAL PRICE
1	96373-3		$16.00	
2	92619-6		$16.00	

Boston Globe Sunday Crosswords
Clever puzzles by Hook, Cox, and Rathvon.

VOL	ISBN	QUANTITY	PRICE	TOTAL PRICE
1	92540-8		$8.50	
2	92539-4		$8.50	
3	92612-9		$8.50	
4	92613-7		$8.50	
5	92746-X		$8.50	

Los Angeles Times Sunday Crosswords
Witty, contemporary puzzles.

VOL	ISBN	QUANTITY	PRICE	TOTAL PRICE
10	92228-X		$8.50	
11	92229-8		$8.50	
12	92230-1		$8.50	
13	92231-X		$8.50	
14	92232-8		$8.50	
15	92788-5		$8.50	

The Washington Post Sunday Crosswords
N.Y. Times-quality puzzles from the nation's capital.

VOL	ISBN	QUANTITY	PRICE	TOTAL PRICE
1	91933-5		$8.50	
2	91934-3		$8.50	
3	92109-7		$8.00	
4	92396-0		$8.50	
5	92648-X		$8.50	

Random House Sunday Crosswords
Intelligent, witty puzzles, a few notches less difficult than the New York Times.

VOL	ISBN	QUANTITY	PRICE	TOTAL PRICE
1	92554-8		$8.50	
2	92766-4		$8.50	

The New York Times Daily Crosswords
America's favorite mental exercise!

VOL	ISBN	QUANTITY	PRICE	TOTAL PRICE
35	92270-0		$8.00	
36	92340-5		$8.50	
37	92358-8		$8.50	
38	92450-9		$8.50	
39	92481-9		$8.50	
40	92538-6		$8.50	
41	92617-X		$8.50	
42	92706-0		$8.50	
43	92760-5		$8.50	
44	92801-6		$8.50	

The New York Times Sunday Crosswords
The standard by which other crosswords have been judged for more than 50 years.

VOL	ISBN	QUANTITY	PRICE	TOTAL PRICE
15	91781-2		$8.50	
16	91839-8		$8.00	
17	91878-9		$8.00	
18	92268-9		$8.50	
19	92083-X		$8.50	
20	92451-7		$8.00	
21	92615-3		$8.50	

Random House Club Crosswords
120 Sunday-size puzzles from America's exclusive clubs.

VOL	ISBN	QUANTITY	PRICE	TOTAL PRICE
1	92638-2		$12.50	

The Puzzlemaster Presents
200 word games from Will Shortz's popular Sunday morning radio show.

VOL	ISBN	QUANTITY	PRICE	TOTAL PRICE
	96386-5		$12.00	

Very Tough Puzzles
The toughest puzzles ever published in book form!
Random House UltraHard Crosswords

VOL	ISBN	QUANTITY	PRICE	TOTAL PRICE
1	96372-5		$8.50	
2	92482-7		$8.50	
3	92701-X		$8.50	

The New York Times Toughest Crosswords

VOL	ISBN	QUANTITY	PRICE	TOTAL PRICE
1	91694-8		$9.00	
2	91828-2		$9.00	
3	91912-2		$9.00	
4	92178-X		$9.00	
5	92618-8		$9.00	

Random House Sunday MegaOmnibus
America's biggest crossword book! 300 Sunday puzzles, edited by Will Weng.

VOL	ISBN	QUANTITY	PRICE	TOTAL PRICE
1	92708-7		$12.50	

Crossword Omnibus Volumes
Each with 200 crosswords, at a great price!
Los Angeles Times Sunday Crossword Omnibus

VOL	ISBN	QUANTITY	PRICE	TOTAL PRICE
1	92758-3		$12.00	

Will Weng Sunday Crossword Omnibus

VOL	ISBN	QUANTITY	PRICE	TOTAL PRICE
1	91300-0		$11.00	
2	91645-X		$11.00	
3	91935-1		$11.00	

The New York Times Daily Crossword Omnibus

VOL	ISBN	QUANTITY	PRICE	TOTAL PRICE
1	91094-X		$10.00	
2	91018-4		$11.00	
3	91066-4		$10.00	
4	91117-2		$11.00	
5	91708-1		$11.00	
6	92124-0		$11.00	
7	92541-6		$11.00	
8	92759-1		$11.00	

The New York Times Sunday Crossword Omnibus

VOL	ISBN	QUANTITY	PRICE	TOTAL PRICE
1	91139-3		$11.00	
2	91791-X		$11.00	
3	91936-X		$11.00	
4	92480-0		$11.00	

The Crossword Answer Book
The most comprehensive crossword reference, guaranteed to have more of the answers you're looking for!

VOL	ISBN	QUANTITY	PRICE	TOTAL PRICE
	92729-X		$27.50	

The New York Times Crossword Dictionary
The revised edition of the classic reference book for crossword fans.

VOL	ISBN	QUANTITY	PRICE	TOTAL PRICE
	92373-1		$27.50	

Parent and Child Puzzles
The only books specially designed for parents and children (ages 8 to 13) to do together.

VOL	ISBN	QUANTITY	PRICE	TOTAL PRICE
1	92543-2		$12.00	
2	92703-6		$12.00	

Acrostic Puzzles
Change-of-pace puzzles with a literary flavor that reveal interesting quotations when completed.
Random House Crostics (All new puzzles!)

VOL	ISBN	QUANTITY	PRICE	TOTAL PRICE
1	92768-0		$8.50	

The New York Times Acrostics

VOL	ISBN	QUANTITY	PRICE	TOTAL PRICE
5	92537-8		$8.50	
6	92620-X		$8.50	

GAMES Magazine Crosswords & Word Games
Lively, solver-friendly puzzles from America's most fascinating puzzle magazine.
World's Most Ornery Crosswords

VOL	ISBN	QUANTITY	PRICE	TOTAL PRICE
	92081-3		$14.00	

The Giant Book of Games

VOL	ISBN	QUANTITY	PRICE	TOTAL PRICE
1	91951-3		$15.00	
2	92614-1		$14.00	

Will Shortz's Best Brain Busters

VOL	ISBN	QUANTITY	PRICE	TOTAL PRICE
	91952-1		$12.00	

Games' Best Pencil Puzzles

VOL	ISBN	QUANTITY	PRICE	TOTAL PRICE
1	92080-5		$12.00	
2	92553-X		$12.00	

Brain Twisters from the World Puzzle Championships

VOL	ISBN	QUANTITY	PRICE	TOTAL PRICE
1	92146-1		$11.00	
2	92616-1		$12.00	

More Puzzles For Kids
Start your favorite youngster on a lifetime of brainbuilding fun! (ages 7 to 14)
GAMES Magazine Kids' Giant Book of Games

VOL	ISBN	QUANTITY	PRICE	TOTAL PRICE
	92199-2		$12.00	

GAMES Magazine Riddlers for Kids

VOL	ISBN	QUANTITY	PRICE	TOTAL PRICE
	92385-5		$11.00	

Cryptic Crosswords
Sophisticated puzzles in the British style, using American English.
Henry Hook's Cryptic Crosswords

VOL	ISBN	QUANTITY	PRICE	TOTAL PRICE
1	92767-2		$11.00	

Random House Guide to Cryptic Crosswords

VOL	ISBN	QUANTITY	PRICE	TOTAL PRICE
	92621-8		$14.00	

Random House Cryptic Crosswords

VOL	ISBN	QUANTITY	PRICE	TOTAL PRICE
1	96371-7		$11.00	
2	92562-9		$10.00	
3	92770-2		$11.00	

GAMES Magazine Cryptic Crosswords

VOL	ISBN	QUANTITY	PRICE	TOTAL PRICE
	91999-8		$8.00	

N.Y. Times Best Diagramless Crosswords
The only series of diagramless crosswords!

VOL	ISBN	QUANTITY	PRICE	TOTAL PRICE
1	92608-0		$8.50	
2	92707-9		$8.50	

Additional Times Books crossword puzzle books are available through your local bookstore, or fill out this coupon and return to:

RANDOM HOUSE, INC., 400 HAHN ROAD, WESTMINSTER, MD 21157. ATTN: ORDER PROCESSING

TO ORDER CALL TOLL-FREE
1-800-793-2665

☐ Enclosed is my check or money order payable to Times Books

☐ Charge my account with: ☐ American Express ☐ Visa ☐ MasterCard

[ ][ ][ ][ ][ ][ ][ ][ ][ ][ ][ ][ ][ ][ ][ ][ ]

EXP DATE (MO/YR)

Please send me copies of the crossword books I have checked off, in the amounts indicated.

Name (please print) _____   Signature _____

Address _____ City _____ State _____ Zip _____

Price applies to U.S. and territories only. In Canada write Random House of Canada, 5390 Ambler Drive, Mississauga, Ontario. (Prices subject to change.)

POSTAGE & HANDLING

TOTAL DOLLARS	ADD
0-$14.99	$3.00
$15.00-$29.99	$4.00
$30.00-$49.99	$6.00
$50.00-$99.99	$10.00

Total Books _____
Total Dollars $ _____
Sales Tax $ _____
(Where applicable)
Postage and Handling $ _____
See chart at left
Total Enclosed $ _____

ANSWERS

7 CAPITAL CITIES TOUR

C	A	N	B	E	R	R	A		W
B	R	A	S	I	L	I	A		E
K	I	N	G	S	T	O	N		L
P	N	O	M	P	E	N	H		L
M	O	N	R	O	V	I	A		I
A	S	U	N	C	I	O	N		N
S	A	N	T	I	A	G	O		G
H	E	L	S	I	N	K	I		T
F	R	E	E	T	O	W	N		O
P	R	E	T	O	R	I	A		N

8 WHAT'S THE POINT

3	3	6	2	3
5	4	3	2	4
5	2	2	0	3
2	2	3	0	2
4	3	5	3	6

8 GEO-LOGICAL

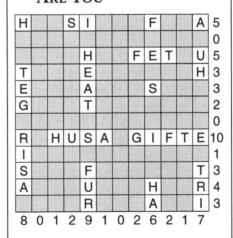

```
            T
            1
        2 1 2 0 0
    1 3 O K O O O 1
      1 Y Y T Y O 0
  0 1 1 T O K Y O 1    K
      0 T T T Y K 1
      1 Y O T K K 2
        1 1 0 3 0
        1
            Y
```

9 INTRODUCTION TO ALBANIAN

B	U	L	M	E	T		U	L	E	M
A	R	A	B		R	O	L		H	A
R	A	K	I	T	I	K		D		R
E	T		Z	E	M	E	R	U	A	R
L	E	R	O	J		R	E	M		E
E		U	T		H		C	E	M	
	E	M	E	R	O	R	E		A	Q
B	U	B	R	E	K		T	A	N	I
A	N		O		E	C	E	S		L
R	U	A	J	T	J	E		H	U	A
I	K	I		I		N	O	T	A	R

10 HOW COORDINATED ARE YOU

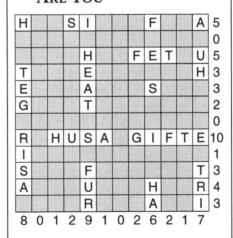

H		S	I			F			A	5
			H		F	E	T		U	0 5
T			E						H	3
E			A			S				3 2
G			T							0
R		H	U	S	A		G	I	F	T E	10
I										1
S	A		F						T	3
A			U			H			R	4 3
			R			A			I	3

8 0 1 2 9 1 0 2 6 2 1 7

11 BATTLE-MINE-SWEEPER-SHIPS

11 FIGURE IT OUT

5	8	4	1		4	3	3	2
2			5	4	1			7
3	1	4	7		6	2	3	9
9		8				2		1
6	3	6	4		9	8	9	6
	2		7	6	2		9	
2	5	6	5		1	8	1	7
9			6	7	3			5
7	1	5	6		6	5	1	0

12 SOMETHING FOR EVERYONE

B	E	L	L		K	E	L	V	I	N	
E	R	O	I	C	A		L	A	S	E	R
N	O		B	A	R	O		L	O	R	D
E	S	P	E	R	A	N	T	O		O	
L		P	R	E	T	O	R	I	A		I
U	R		I		E		O	S	C	A	R
X	A	M	A	X		N	P		C	I	A
	M	O		C	O	O	P	E	R		N
H	A	R	T		D	V	O	R	A	K	
U		S	O	F	I	A		A		O	M
O	R	E	G	O	N			I	T	O	A
T	A		O	X		C	R	O	S	B	Y

13 DO RE MI

I	R	R		K	O	P	F		G	I
C	O	L	T		T	U	L	P	E	N
H	S		A	U		P	A	A	R	E
T	A	U	B		S	P	U	R		R
H		H	A	L	T	E		T	O	T
Y	T		K	A	I		S	E	E	
O	J	E		S	C	H	U	R	K	E
L	A	T	S	C	H		F	R	O	N
O		A	C	H		O	F	E	N	
G	F		H	E	U		I		O	B
E	T	U	I		M	A	X	I	M	E

C	A	R	L

O	R	F	F

14 Division of Labor

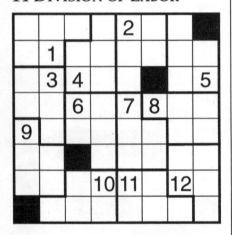

(Grid with numbers 1–12)

16-17 Mosaic

14 Urban Skyline

	4↓		3↓		
5	3	6	1	2	4
3	4	5	2	6	1
4	5	1	6	3	2
2	6	4	5	1	3
1	2	3	4	5	6
6	1	2	3	4	5

3⇒ (row 3), 6⇒ (row 5), 1⇒ (row 6)
⇐3 (row 3), ⇐3 (row 4), ⇐2 (row 6)
↑3 ↑5 ↑4 (bottom)

15 A Neutral Puzzle

P	A	L	A	D	I	N	■	E	L	E	V	A	G	E
A	S	E	N	■	M	O	C	H	E	■	I	D	O	L
L	Y	Z	E	U	M					T	R	A	E	G	E
A	L	A	■	N	E			T	U	■	P	O	T
Z	■	R	H	I	N			E	T	A	T	■	T
Z	E	D	E	R	■		■		A	V	O	I	R
O	N						S	O
■	T						O	■
U	R						L	E
M	O	U	L	E	■		■	A	L	T	A	R
F	■	N	O	C	E		F	R	A	U	■	I
R	O	I	■	O	R		A	D	■	L	O	G
A	D	O	P	T	E		L	U	C	I	D	E
G	E	N	E	■	D	R	E	S	S	■	O	P	E	R
E	N	E	R	G	I	E	■	T	O	R	C	E	R	E

18 Coming or Going

T	W	A	I	N		P	U	C	C	I	N	I
I		N		E		O		H				B
T		D		W		E	R	A	S	M	U	S		E
O	B	E	R	T	H			P		E		N
	R		O		B		L	E	N	I	N
H	U	S		N	U	R	M	I		U
A		E			O		N	E	H	R	U
L	I	N	C	O	L	N			I		S
L			C		T		M	A	N	E	T		I
E		F		A	B	E	L		R		N
Y	E	A	T	S		A	R	A	G	O	N		O
	L		E		N		G		V
K	E	L	L	Y		A	G	N	O	N

88

19 LABYRINTH

C	U	R	I	E	■	O	S	M	A	N
S	H	A	W	■	M	O	Z	A	R	T
C	O	R	N	E	I	L	L	E	■	E
H	U	G	O	■	M	E	N	D	E	L
H	■	S	P	I	E	L	B	E	R	G
C	A	E	S	A	R	■	B	O	H	R
S	H	A	K	E	S	P	E	A	R	E
S	C	H	I	L	L	E	R	■	D	
■	E	I	N	S	T	E	I	N	■	D
E	N	D	O	■	D	A	R	W	I	N
H	O	M	E	R	■	S	T	E	I	N

20 ORDER, ORDER

1	4	2	3

21 TURN, TURN, TURN

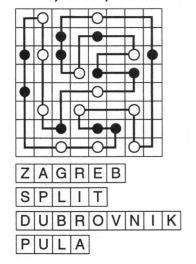

Z	A	G	R	E	B
S	P	L	I	T
D	U	B	R	O	V	N	I	K
P	U	L	A

22 BLOCK PARTY

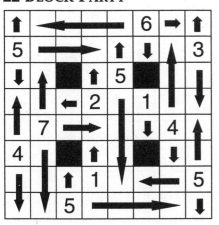

22 IN-EQUALITIES

4	<	5	=	5	>	4	>	1
v		v		v		v		^
3	>	2	>	1	<	3	>	2
v		v		^		v		II
2	>	1	<	3	>	1	<	2
II		^		^		^		^
2	<	5	>	4	>	2	<	3
^		v		^		^		^
3	<	4	<	5	=	5	>	4

23 LET'S GO TO THE MOVIES

R	E	D	F	O	R	D
D	A	G	O	V	E	R
B	O	U	R	V	I	L
A	N	D	R	E	W	S
R	O	B	E	R	T	S
P	R	E	S	L	E	Y
C	O	S	T	N	E	R
D	O	U	G	L	A	S
M	C	Q	U	E	E	N
W	I	D	M	A	R	K
C	H	A	P	L	I	N

24 MARGINALLY ACCEPTABLE

E	I	N	S	T	E	I	N	N	E	W	T	O
E	G	S	N	I	S	E	E	E	N	A	N	N
R	E	A	S	22/43	B	E	L	22/34	G	I	N	G
A	A	23/25	P	A	T	33/55	N	E	K	32/52	N	O
E	D	L	G	44/44	G	O	L	44/44	G	O	S	E
P	U	25/23	K	O	T	55/33	R	E	G	52/32	C	T
S	E	A	T	43/22	R	U	I	34/22	U	R	E	H
E	L	H	E	E	I	G	C	S	E	T	O	E
K	A	H	S	N	E	V	O	H	T	E	E	B

25 DRINKING SPREE

T	H	R	I	L	L	■	A	R	C	H	■
A	R	D	U	O	U	S	■	O	■	C	E
I	M	M	E	M	O	R	I	A	L	■	H
B	A	N	■	S	P	A	■	I	D	E	A
L	U	S	T	■	E	U	N	U	C	H	S
R	■	I	N	N	S	■	G	■	L	T	
A	G	A	T	E	■	H	E	A	R	T	Y
E	P	I	G	R	A	M	■	U	T	■	E
E	R	■	E	M	O	T	I	O	N	A	L
S	■	S	I	E	S	T	A	■	R	A	M

The before clues are entered across.
The after clues zig-zag from top to
bottom in random fashion.

26 FOLLOWING DIRECTIONS

S ↓	5 ↓	8 ↓	4 ←
12 →	13 ↓	10 →	11 ←
2 →	6 →	7 ↑	3 ↑
1 ↑	14 →	9 ↑	★

27 MEET YOU 'ROUND THE CORNER

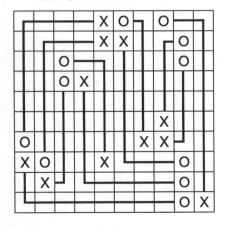

28 URBAN GRIDLOCK

P	O	S	A	K	A	D	E	T	R	O	I	T
A	D	E	N	P	N	O	M	P	E	N	H	E
R	E	Y	K	J	A	V	I	K	I	A	A	H
I	S	W	A	N	S	E	A	K	M	S	R	E
S	S	B	R	O	S	R	M	O	S	T	A	R
P	A	R	A	M	A	R	I	B	O	I	R	A
A	P	I	A	S	U	E	Z	E	S	S	E	N
L	U	S	A	K	A	D	A	L	L	A	S	T
E	E	B	Y	C	M	N	G	Y	O	R	I	O
R	D	A	S	A	M	A	R	K	A	N	D	K
M	A	N	I	L	A	R	E	U	F	A	O	I
O	M	E	D	I	N	A	B	X	B	R	N	O

29 WRITERS BLOCK

G	D	R	A	G	U	D			H	Y
A	L	A	R	T	S	I	M	A	E	
L	N		S	H	C	A	S	M	A	
S	E	L	A	X	N	E	S	S	T	
W	S	W		N	C	A	M	U	S	
O	N	E	I	L	L		O	N	E	
R	E	O		E	S	S	E	H	S	
T	J	A	N	D	R	I	C		Y	
H	E	D	I	G	T	O	I	L	E	H
Y	R	O	L	L	A	N	D		H	

K	I	P	L	I	N	G

30 EDISON

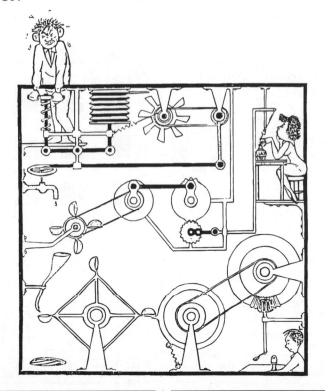

31 4 x 4

23	31	12	44
42	14	33	21
34	22	41	13
11	43	24	32

31 EASY AS...

		A				
B	B				B	A
B			B	C		C
	B	C			A	C
	A		C	A	C	B
A	A			C		

32 WHO'S WHO

A	KI	H	I	TO	S	H	ERI	DAN
KE	PL	ER	DE	SC	ART	E		TE
M	ING	ZO	L	A	R	USS	E	LL
A	RA	G	O	N	I	E	TZ	S	CHE
LA	W	MA	N	N	■	■	A	R
T	LI	ND	ER	I	■		KI	M
A	NG	ELA	I	GOR	■		PER	ON
TÜR	S	HA	K	E	S	PE	AR	E
K	ANT	VEL	DE	D	UE	RER	PAD	T

33 CRYPTO-CROSS-SUM

R	A	Y	B	N	T	I	H	L	O
1	2	3	4	5	6	7	8	9	0

	13	12	17	30		35	12	8	9
30	7	8	9	6	11	5	1	3	2
20	6	4	1	9	23	8	3	5	7
20	6\12	7	5	17\	9	8	9	21
4	3	1	18\20	7	5	6	6\27	2	4
45	9	2	4	3	1	7	5	6	8
13	8	3	2	11	7\12	2	1	9
5	14\11	6	8	5	1	4	17	9
16	4	6	5	1	21	2	7	9	3
11	1	5	3	2	27	4	9	8	6

90

34 THIS:THAT

```
S T A R T ■ P A N A M A ■
P E L E ■ E R O I C A ■ C
I S ■ N A S A ■ C ■ O T O
E L D O R A D O ■ B ■ L U
L A ■ I M ■ O S C A R ■ L
B ■ G R A F ■ M I K A D O
E C U ■ D I V A ■ U ■ E M
R E A G A N ■ N L ■ K G B
G ■ R I ■ N R ■ U E F A
■ E N D O ■ E F T A ■ S M
G R E E N W I C H ■ O ■ ■
K O R ■ O H M ■ E S A K I
■ S I D ■ O S I R I S ■ N
```

35 A CAPITAL IDEA

```
A S B C U H R T E
U R H E T B S A C
E C T A R S B H U
T A S B E U C R H
B U C H A R E S T
H E R S C T U B A
S B U T H C A E R
C H E R S A T U B
R T A U B E H C S
```

35 REACH FOR THE STARS

```
      2 2 1 1 3 2 2 2
3  ✶ ↓ →   ✶ →   ✶
1      ↓ →   ✶
2    ✶ ↖   ✶ ↗ ↑
1  ↘     ✶ ↘   ↙ ↑
2    ✶ ↗   → ✶   ↙
3  ✶ → ↓   ✶ ↖ ✶ ↓
1    ✶ ↑ ↑   ←
2  ↑ ↗     → ✶   ✶
```

36 ALCHEMY

```
G A P E R S T R E S S
O M A N E U R O S E E
N O T [Ai] V A [Ag] B R A N D
G A R N I Z O E [N5] T E
A L O O S U I R E I S
S I [Na] S A L N O O R S
E N [Cl] E R U S A N T I
N E I [G3] E N A L G E N
T A P U N A N I E M [Ca]
A R E N D V O S L E S
[R2] I M B O E B O E R [O4]
```

1 2 3 4 5 = ARGON

37 CHECKMATE

```
O R F ■ N E B I
N E ■ T A ■ A ■
E F O R ■ A T A
M U F E S S I R
■ J ■ T A T ■ D
I ■ B E L ■ Y A
K A R ■ I M A L
A L E Y H ■ S A
```

```
I K I ■ A K C A
K I ■ O D ■ A ■
I R A T ■ U T U
Z A R A R S I Z
■ Z ■ R E T ■ U
D ■ L I F ■ A N
I D U ■ A H I T
T A M A H ■ T U
```

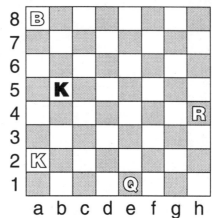

38 THREE ON A MATCH

```
C E L S I U S
N I A G A R A
A S T A I R E
A K I H I T O
P O T S D A M
C H A (P) L I N
A L L (E) G R O
A T L (A) N T A
F I S (C) H E R
S A L (E) R N O
T R I S T A N
H A R V A R D
C O L O G N E
D O M I N G O
T A L L I N N
```

39 THE HEIGHT OF PUZZLING

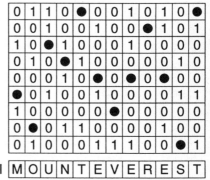

```
0 1 1 0 ● 0 0 1 0 1 0 ●
0 0 1 0 0 1 0 0 ● 1 0 1
1 0 ● 1 0 0 0 1 0 0 0 0
0 1 0 ● 1 0 0 0 0 0 1 0
0 0 0 1 0 ● 0 ● 0 ● 0 0
● 0 1 0 0 1 0 0 0 0 1 1
1 0 0 0 0 0 ● 0 0 0 0 0
0 ● 0 1 1 0 0 0 0 1 0 0
0 1 0 0 0 1 1 0 0 ● 0 1
```

I | M O U N T E V E R E S T

II | 8 | 8 | 4 | 8 |

The height of Mount Everest is 8,848m.

41 MADE IN THE SHADE

0	1	2	3	3	2	1
1	2	2	2	2	1	1
1	2	5	5	4	2	1
2	3	3	1	1	0	0
1	2	5	5	4	2	1
1	2	2	2	2	1	1
1	3	5	6	6	4	2
2	2	4	3	4	2	2
3	3	6	3	6	3	3
2	1	3	1	3	1	2
2	3	4	3	4	3	2
2	2	3	2	2	1	1
3	3	5	3	3	2	1
2	1	2	0	0	0	0
2	3	4	3	3	2	1
2	2	3	2	3	2	2
3	3	5	3	5	3	3
2	1	2	0	2	1	2
2	3	4	3	4	3	2
2	2	3	2	3	2	2
3	4	7	6	7	4	3
2	2	3	2	3	2	2
2	4	6	6	6	4	2
1	1	2	2	3	2	2
2	4	6	6	7	4	3
1	1	2	2	4	3	3
2	4	6	6	6	4	2
1	1	2	2	3	2	2
2	4	6	6	6	4	2
2	2	4	3	4	2	2
3	3	6	3	6	3	3
2	1	3	1	3	1	2
1	1	1	0	1	1	1

42 OUT OF AFRICA

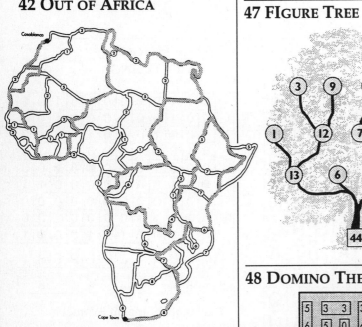

43 CAN YOU DIGIT?

923
394
529

44 FRUIT SALAD

6 APPLES

45 NESSIE

46 BUILDING BLOCKS

8 + 12
11 + 14

47 FIGURE TREE

Tree connecting numbered nodes:
3, 9, 5, 2, 8
1, 12, 7, 4, 10
13, 6, 11, 14
44

48 DOMINO THEORY

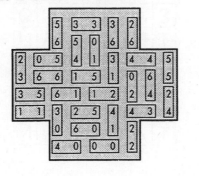

49 PENTOMINOS

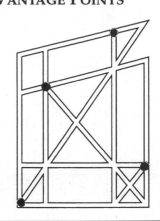

Right side clues: 8, 5, 4, 4, 3, 10, 1, 3, 6, 5, 5, 6
Bottom clues: 5 7 5 3 6 6 5 2 5 5

50 VANTAGE POINTS

51 POLITICAL ASYLUM

MACHIAVELLI

H	S	I	L	I	T	O	M	I	K	S
Z	R	A	J	C	N	N	C	R	O	G
A	A	R	A	N	C	E	I	E	I	S
R	A	L	I	O	U	M	A	H	M	E
V	I	E	R	K	B	H	R	L	B	A
N	O	E	V	A	Z	L	E	D	H	R
A	A	C	U	S	N	C	H	N	K	V
T	F	A	E	A	A	M	C	P	A	R
Z	C	O	M	E	O	E	K	K	L	A
L	T	L	S	D	A	A	I	O	S	O
C	O	I	O	M	R	I	V	A	Y	K

K	O	H	L	
G	O	N	C	Z
R	E	I	N	A
M	O	I		
H	A	V	E	L
Z	H	E	L	E	V
K	U	C	A	N
A	R	A	F	A	T
K	O	K		
A	S	S	A	D
K	O	V	A	C

A	C	L	M	M	B	M	C	P	B	S
Z	A	I	A	E	R	E	H	R	I	O
N	S	L	J	K	U	N	I	O	Y	A
A	T	I	O	S	T	E	R	D	A	R
R	R	C	R	I	O	M	A	I		E
	O			N			C			S

52 VALUE ADDED

A	B	C	D	E	F	G	H	I
8	5	3	1	4	6	7	2	9

53 SYMBOLISM

$$3808 \ - \ 1450 \ = \ 2358$$

3808	−	1450	=	2358
÷		+		−
17	x	38	=	646
=		=		=
224	+	1488	=	1712

A	B	C	D	E	F	G	H	I
3	8	0	1	4	5	2	7	6

54 JIGSAW LETTERS

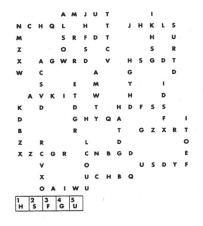

1	2	3	4	5
H	S	F	G	U

55 WEATHER WATCH

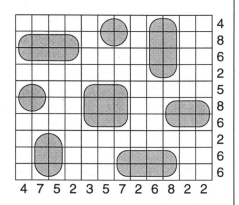

56 FIGURE FINDER

624

57 PILLBOX

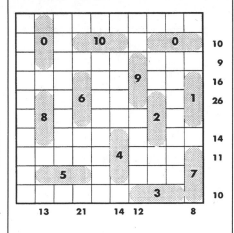

58 MINESWEEPER

59 BUILDING BLOCKS
(PART II)

60-61 NUMBER GRID

A

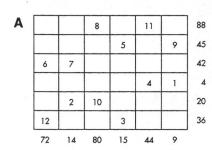

B

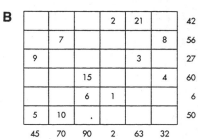

C

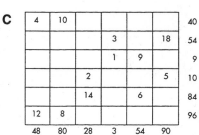

D

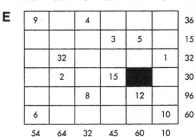

E

62-65 CANALSIDE HOUSES

66-69 BATTLESHIPS

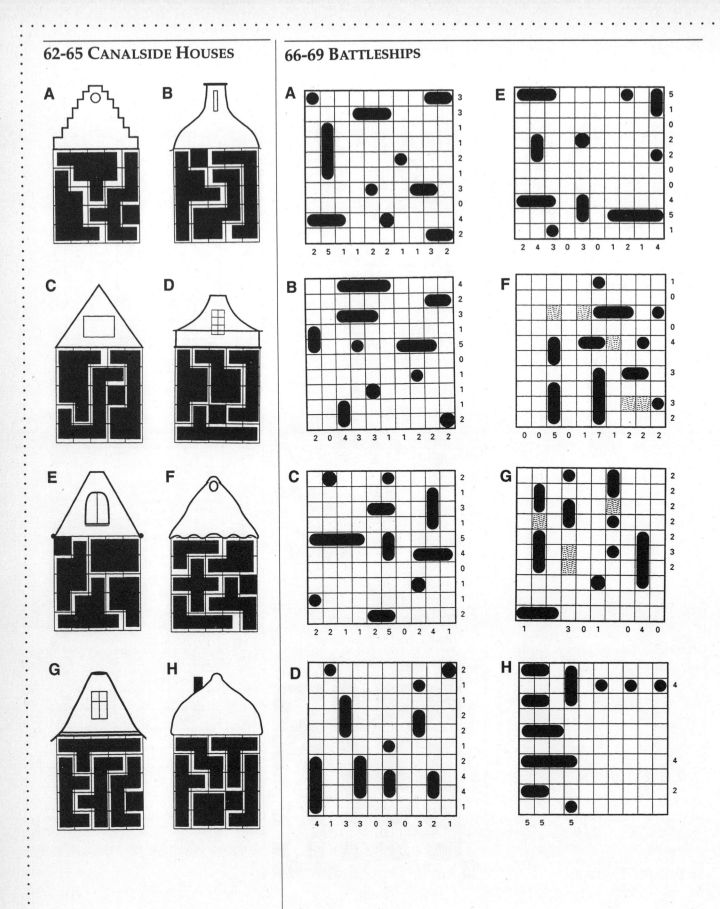

94

70 CROSS SUMS

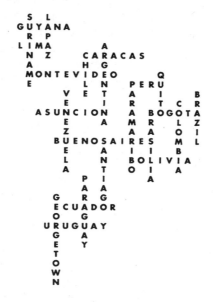

71 ONE-WAY TRAFFIC

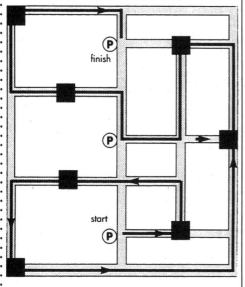

72 THE BEST SITES

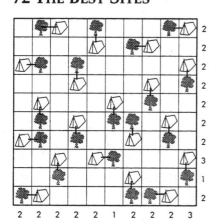

73 WORDS ACROSS SOUTH AMERICA

74 SUMS OF SYMBOLS

♠ = 4
♥ = 6
♦ = 2
♣ = 1

75 EASY AS... (PART II)

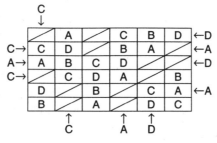

76 ANY WAY YOU CAN

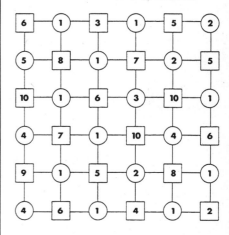

77 CIRCLES AND SQUARES

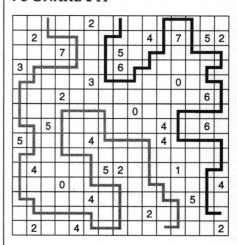

78 SNAKE PIT

95

79 E-Mail

80 Out of Africa (Part II)

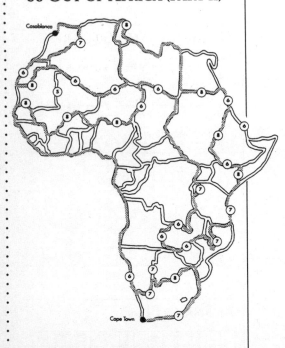

81 Figure Square

2	6	3	1	4	5
5	1	6	3	2	4
1	2	4	6	5	3
4	3	1	5	6	2
6	4	5	2	3	1
3	5	2	4	1	6

82 Put the Pictures in the Right ORder

The correct solution is D-F-A-C-E-B.

The "story": man cuts two pieces of cake and puts them on plates (D). Then he makes coffee, using the machine (F). While the coffee drips, he puts food in the cat's dish (A). The cat dives into the food; the man cannot contain himself either and eats two pieces of cake (C). By now, the coffee is ready. He pours the coffee (E). Finally, the man cuts two new pieces of cake (B).

CREDITS

FOURTH WORLD PUZZLE CHAMPIONSHIP

The puzzles on pages 7 through 39 are courtesy of Ovidiu Sperlea of Rebus Labarint, Brasov, Romania.

FIFTH WORLD PUZZLE CHAMPIONSHIP

The puzzles on pages 41 through 82 are courtesy of Rob Geensen of Puzzelsport (Vitgeverij paarnestad BV), Hamlen, the Netherlands.